To Uncle Buckie -

From Terry and Linda

MW00635349

1997

Merry Christmas!

With more Love than you can ever imagine.

Linda

25 Years

*ACTUALLY 26½ YEARS BUT 25 YEARS ALLOW ME TO USE THE NEAT SILVERY COLOR ON THE COVER.

The editorial cartoons and arts of Clyde Wells

Introductions by targeted public officials, past and present

The Augusta Chronicle
NEWS BUILDING
AUGUSTA, GEORGIA 30913

Published by Morris Communications Corporation

To Emily,
my Granddaughter

This is not a work of fiction. Names, characters, places, and incidents are neither the product of the author's imagination nor are they used fictitiously, and any resemblance to actual persons, living or dead, events, or locales is entirely intentional.

If you purchase this book without a cover you should be aware that this book may have been stolen property and reported as "unsold and destroyed" to the publisher. In such case neither the author nor the publisher has received any payment for this "stripped book." It is generally believed that this is the origin of the term "being ripped off."

Library of Congress Cataloging-in-Publication Data

Wells, Clyde, 1934-

Wells 25* years : the editorial cartoons and arts of Clyde Wells / introductions by targeted public officials, past and present.
p. cm.
"Actually 26 1/2 years but 25 years allow me to use the neat silvery color on the cover."
ISBN 0-9618270-9-2
1. Editorial cartoons--United States. 2. American wit and humor, Pictorial. I. Title.
NC1429.W4495A4 1997
741.5'973--dc21 97-31401
CIP

Printed by Streeter Printing & Graphics, Inc.

Augusta, Georgia 30901

author's note

Never lean into a left hook. It's an old saying, and a wise one, that I chose to ignore in inviting 39 present and past public officials (entertainer James Brown being the sole exception) to write the introductions to this book. To my surprise, 29 responded. I would have been happy with half that number. My original layout included two or three pages for introductions. Instead, I needed nearly seven pages. I was further astonished that the overwhelming number were complimentary. In my invitation I wrote that they could say whatever they wished about me and/or my work and I would not reply with a "last crack," so to speak. Some of the more complimentary comments came from those I had persistently targeted over the years. Complimentary enough to almost cause regret for some of my more, shall we say, ungracious shots. (The operative word being 'almost'.)

That said, this book is my swan song as editorial cartoonist for *The Augusta Chronicle*. My first cartoon was in March 1971 and I retire at the end of 1997, almost 27 years. I enjoyed much of it. In the early years, the local power structure, both political and business, seemed amused by my work. In 1975 I was presented a plaque by the Richmond County Board of Commissioners engraved "in recognition of the cunning humor he has added to the political life of Richmond County." But somewhere about halfway, they realized that I wasn't just providing comic relief for the readers of the *Chronicle's* editorial pages. Editorial cartoons are satire. Satire is defined as follows; trenchant wit, irony, or sarcasm used to expose and discredit vice or folly! The cartoons were meant to prod the powerful to do the right thing and restrain them in dubious and sometimes nefarious undertakings in conducting the public's business. That they were Democrat or Republican, Liberal or Conservative, Black or White, Man or Woman was irrelevant to me. Only whether they were right or wrong mattered. In many of their views, it was unwarranted and unfair criticism. I drew the warts and not the good side. Editorials and columns more than adequately handle the praise and compliments. Editorial cartoons criticize – that is the nature of the beast. The goal — to curtail the abuse of power. I believe the public was the better served by my work. Obviously, there is room for disagreement. I haven't received many plaques in these later years.

This is the third book featuring my work. *The Net Effect* covered the 1970s and *The Clyde Wells Cartoon Book* the 1980s. Some of those cartoons are included in this book, but the emphasis is on the 1990s. Included are 695 cartoons and drawings, about ten percent of my output over the years. I selected what I considered my best work, both as to the drawing and the commentary. In addition to the editorial cartoons are portrait drawings of sports and political figures and a few other sundry etchings. Near the end of the book are a few examples of *Go Figure*, my attempt at producing a comic strip. It ran for 40 weeks during 1995 in the *Chronicle* Sunday color comics. King Features offered to syndicate the strip but only if I provided it on a daily basis. At my advanced age I decided I could not handle this added burden to my regular task of drawing editorial cartoons. The two projects could have had me actually spending full working days at my drawing board! *Go Figure* may crop up again in my retirement years.

In the final analysis, anyone dispensing his work and talent to the general public must feel he has their approval and support. Otherwise the work will not be enjoyable and probably not successful. I feel I have had that approval and support over the past 26 plus years. I appreciate that.

Clyde Wells
October, 1997

introductions

In retrospect, I remember providing you with ample grist for your cartoonist skills (which are among the best I have ever seen). During the tumultuous '70s, I was the frequent target of your harpooning. I never felt, however, that you did not present a viable viewpoint, no matter how "unfair, overly critical, too harsh, too flippant." In that vein, you were true to your profession. The Augusta body politic was the better for it.

Anthony A. Alaimo

Judge, U.S. District Court, Southern District of Georgia

Being featured in a Clyde Wells cartoon is something that all local politicians enjoy, whether they admit it or not.

When I first ran for the Richmond County Commission in 1978, one of my campaign managers, Finley Merry, bribed Clyde to draw a cartoon of me before I was elected and gave it to me for my birthday. I was thrilled. After that there were some that were actually published with about ten percent showing me in a good light.

I was so happy to be included in Clyde's first book, *The Net Effect*, I bought ten copies and gave them to my family for Christmas presents. Since then I've found that my out-of-town relatives are more appreciative of ties, socks, and underwear.

I'm honored to have been speared with that sharp, vicious Clyde Wells pen, but I can't say that I miss it.

Now that you're being put out to pasture, I hope Billy Morris gives you the best stall at Creek Plantation.

Frank Albert

Former Richmond County Commissioner, former Georgia state senator, District 23

Retirement is something to be celebrated. Especially when it's yours! Certainly I will miss your penetrating cartoons about others; they were consistently on target and frequently funny. But I won't miss those that featured me. For some unknown reason, they were the only ones consistently wrong and frequently humorless! Nobody is perfect, I guess.

To tell the truth, though (a special talent of a politician), even those about me brought an occasional chuckle. They may even have caused me to rethink a position or action — at least momentarily.

The cartoonist's pen can be a mighty sword, even a cruel one at times. But in a democracy based on free speech, the cartoon is the most concise example of that freedom. I congratulate you on having wielded your pen so ably for so many years. And I pledge to conduct myself in such a manner so as never to tempt you to come out of retirement.

Best wishes.

Thomas F. Allgood, Sr.

Board of Regents, former Georgia state senator, District 22

I am pleased and honored to be requested to offer this foreword to the third publication of my friend Clyde Wells.

Yes, Clyde is well known nationally as one of the most imaginative, innovative, courageous and artistically talented cartoonists in the United States. His celebrated work has been appreciated by many public figures including presidents of the United States, members of Congress, governors, athletes, and of course, local citizens of Augusta that have been in the limelight.

You would wonder why someone like me, who has often been the subject of some of his creative cartoons, would appreciate being a contributor to this foreword. As a former politician I certainly did not appreciate being singled out from time to time in some outlandish manner, but I was never offended, because Clyde was always fair, and I understood the purpose of his satire. One particular cartoon that was meaningful to me was the cartoon depicting the John C. Calhoun Expressway at its temporary terminus at 15th Street, with an exaggerated "net" to catch the cars as they drove off. At the time I was a member of the Board of the State Department of Transportation. This cartoon was outlandish, but true, and was a great stimulus to get me more active to see that this highway was finished to its planned location. While it was not finished until I was a member of Congress from this area, I never forgot this cartoon, or its message.

Clyde was more than a cartoonist at *The Augusta Chronicle* — he was also a member of the Editorial Board. As a member of Congress, I had the opportunity on many occasions to appear before the Editorial Board, and I always found Clyde as an informed, educated, and intellectual interrogator. His contributions to his profession was even more than his artistic talent.

I am sure that I express the sentiments of many of our citizens that his retirement will not mean the complete absence of his work locally or nationwide.

Doug Barnard, Jr.

Former congressman (D-Ga.) 10th District

Thank you for your kind invitation to write a foreword for your next book. The fact is, I consider myself fortunate to write a foreword for your next book. The fact is, I consider myself fortunate to be among those you termed to be "a select group of present and former public officials" who have been extended this honor.

When you featured me in my very first cartoon, you compared me to "Carrie Nation" and showed me closing all the bars on election day. I then managed to stay clean and absent from your pen until I began working with the County Commission, a group which always was one of your favorite subjects.

I have enjoyed your "editorial cartoons" for many years, including those directed toward me. Although I appeared to be rather "broad hipped with droopy socks" in a particular edition, I must confess that I chuckle each time I look at it. (However, for the record, I never wear droopy socks!) Actually, I never felt that I had attained success in county government until I was the finished product of your pen. I had finally arrived. I was now a full fledged member of a very select group of individuals including presidents, vice presidents, senators, Congress members, state officials and local officials. Besides, you really didn't have many "females" you could pick on in government, so I was the likely candidate.

I marvel at your creativity, ability and brilliant insight to place before the public your unique view of happenings taking place in government. Although I can't say that I've always agreed with your message, I will admit that you captured the attention of your readers, provoking discussion of the issue of the day. That ability has truly been a service to the community. This collection, I am sure, will rekindle memories of many episodes in the life of Augusta-Richmond County.

Happy retirement.

Linda W. Beazley

Former Richmond County Administrator

Clyde Wells is retiring and some will be happy and others sad. As for me, I have mixed emotions. Clyde possesses the unique ability to understand the issues in our community, state and nation. But, his talent is crafting a cartoon which gets to the heart of the issue while being funny. At least I always thought them funny when they were about those I disagreed with and not so funny when they included me in a critical way. These were the few times that I felt Clyde missed the mark. Clyde Wells will be missed and I wish him well in his retirement.

Bob Beckham

Former Georgia state representative

Your technical and artistic output has always been outstanding and entertaining. However, I feel I should not comment on your choice of subject matter or the general attitude taken toward your subjects. A serious and thoughtful critique of that would be like trying to examine Charlie McCarthy if the ground rules prevented the mention of Edgar Bergen!

Thank you for your cartoons regarding local table tennis. They were most helpful in making this area and Augusta State College a leader in that sport!

Herb Beckham

Former Richmond County School Board member, former Richmond County Commissioner

Thank you for the opportunity to respond to your work. I am honored that you chose to include in your book one of the cartoons you drew during my term of office.

Overall you have an incredible talent for capturing the essence of a political moment. One of the most moving cartoons I have ever seen is your depiction of the Challenger crew flying into the hands of God.

I do, however, have a concern which relates to my own situation and that of other public figures who are subjects of your cartoons. While the cartoon presents one opinion on an event, there is rarely an opportunity "for the rest of the story" to be told.

There is always background information which, for a variety of reasons, is not or cannot be publicized. It is regrettable that public figures are often judged, not by the work that they do, but by the publicity the receive.

I look forward to adding your new book to my collection.

Lynn Cadle

Former Columbia County School Superintendent

Clyde Wells is one of the best political cartoonists. He has given us 27 years of biting humor and insight, defining, in just a few strokes of his pen, the essence of complex issues and the manifold ironies of public life, especially as seen from the South.

Jimmy Carter

Former governor of Georgia, former president of the United States

As a public official with a reputation of speaking his mind, the idea of awakening every morning to the prospect of bad press in the daily newspaper is one that is certainly not foreign to me. And when your hometown paper has a political cartoonist as adept at furnishing a zinger as anyone, that prospect becomes ever more possible and usually probable. For the more than 30 years that I have been in public life, this has been the case, for very few in the business of editorial cartoons have been so talented and masterful at providing a succinct commentary within a few copy inches as Clyde Wells.

Clyde Wells' cartoons have been, with few exceptions, a joy to read. His great wit and biting humor are evident in every cartoon he has drawn, and his belief in laying it all on the table has made us kindred spirits. Although our views did not always parallel, I respected his work, for it accurately illustrated his beliefs and communicated a strong message. His pictures certainly conveyed a thousand words, and more importantly provoked thought, which is essential when dealing with issues of public interest.

More than any other medium, editorial cartoons have the ability to say so much so quickly, and in Clyde Wells, the Augusta community was blessed with a true master at his craft. Although it is true that Clyde Wells' work has, at times, brought my blood to boil, his impending retirement comes for me not as a time of rejoice but of sadness, for I consider him a friend. His work will be missed, but I am thankful that we will have this collection to keep as a remembrance of a great career.

Don Cheeks

Georgia state senator, District 23

Clyde Wells' cartoons are, to our community, what those wavy mirrors are to the patrons of the county fair. As the svelte debutante steps before the carnival mirrors, she may be surprised by the rotund reflection. As the lifelong butterball steps up to the magic glass, he may find the tall, strapping image inspiring but, in reality, one he may never see in his own mirror.

Ever since Clyde began lampooning public figures, Augustans have pondered how we would be depicted if we should find ourselves in the cross hair of the cartoonist's pen. Some of us have had the dubious honor of "stepping up to the mirror" – to become the subject of old-fashioned, pictorial satire at its best.

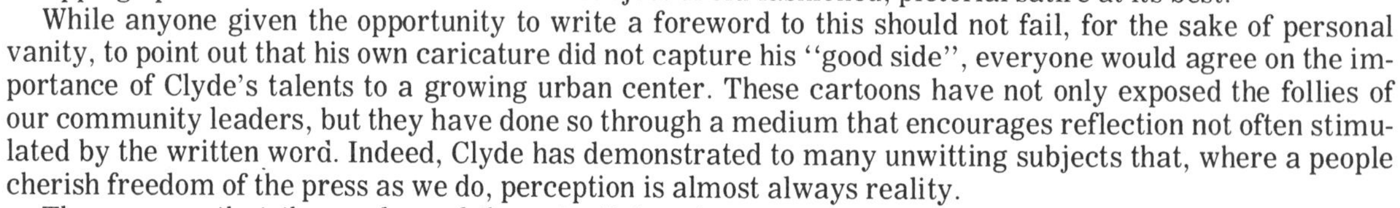

While anyone given the opportunity to write a foreword to this should not fail, for the sake of personal vanity, to point out that his own caricature did not capture his "good side", everyone would agree on the importance of Clyde's talents to a growing urban center. These cartoons have not only exposed the follies of our community leaders, but they have done so through a medium that encourages reflection not often stimulated by the written word. Indeed, Clyde has demonstrated to many unwitting subjects that, where a people cherish freedom of the press as we do, perception is almost always reality.

The concern that the readers of the potential cartoon may perceive it as fact rather than satire, has caused many public servants to avoid impulsive behavior, reflect on the consequences of certain choices, plan more carefully, and articulate better. I, like many, have seen those days when I preferred to be depicted in a better light and protested privately of "unfairness" and "distortion". But, if we are the leaders we fashion ourselves to be, and if we have the resolve to serve honestly and fairly, then the satirical sting is temporary – just like that brief moment before the wavy mirror.

Daniel J. Craig

Augusta Judicial Circuit District Attorney

So, Clyde Wells is finally retiring and he is giving his victims, I mean subjects, the chance to write about him for a change. I know that many politicians would relish this opportunity and many others will breathe a lot easier knowing that he will not have a sketchbook in his hands — at least for print. Having been in the Augusta political world for over 15 years, I have certainly provided my share of material for Clyde. I have laughed at many of his cartoons, I have been hurt by a few. I thought some were fair and that some went a bit too far. Occasionally, I have even planned the perfect murder after one or two cartoons were printed. However, one must admit that Clyde Wells has a great talent in the difficult business of getting a message across to the reading public by way of a single drawing in a very limited space. With Clyde, like it or not, there was usually no question as to the message or person that was the subject of his talent.

Clyde Wells, through his work, has demonstrated almost daily why it is so important for the public to be informed and how we remind our elected officials that the voters are still the bosses. That is why it is easy to write this foreword. It is an opportunity to wish Clyde well in his retirement, but it is also an opportunity to remind all those who read and enjoy this book that it represents our constitutional First Amendment guarantees of freedom of speech and freedom of the press. It is the backbone of our Bill of Rights and without it the United States of America would simply not be the same as we know it today.

Thanks for all the entertainment (at least, almost all, with a couple of well-chosen exceptions!) and enjoy your retirement — so long as you do not have a pen in your hand!

Charles A. DeVaney

Former mayor of Augusta

When I think back over the years of enjoying your cartoons in *The Chronicle*, I am struck by two things:
How often you got it right when cartooning other persons, and how, whenever I was the target, you were completely wrong.
Isn't my observation interesting?

Michael C. Eubanks
Former District Attorney, Augusta Judicial Circuit

Clyde Wells enjoys the reputation of being one of the finest cartoonists, if not the finest, in this state. Although I don't always agree with him, I respect his right of free speech. I can say he doesn't play favorites with his acerbic comments or scurrilous drawings.
One of the few people he has not castigated is his wife!

William M. Fleming, Jr.
Judge of the Superior Courts of the Augusta Judicial Circuit

I have enjoyed many of the editorial cartoons published under your byline over the years. The humor, pathos, and insight interestingly reflect your opinions on the deeds and misdeeds of mankind.
While I realize that public figures must have thick skin and an acceptance of criticism, the situations you "editorialize" should be true and accurate in their depiction. When the drawings attack individuals in a mean-spirited or untruthful manner, I just consider the source.
Thank you for the opportunity to express my opinion as you so freely and regularly do.

Don A. Grantham
Former Richmond County Commissioner

Every once in a while, God taps individuals and endows them with special talents. I believe God did that with Clyde Wells because he is a truly unique cartoonist. Through his cartoons, he has enlightened people on a variety of issues and problems that confront us. His cartoons have reached many communities and have played a major role in shaping and reshaping thousands of reader's minds.
Sometimes, I vehemently disagreed with the cartoons he did on others as well as myself. On the other hand, however, I thought many of his pictorial commentaries were right on target. Knowing Clyde as I do, I am convinced that he always thought that his cartoons did exactly what he intended – served the public interest. Whether they did or not, one thing is certain; they always made us think.
I am sure that this gifted artist could have left Augusta many times for greater professional advancements, but he chose to stay and his staying in Augusta made a tremendous impact upon the public's reaction to a variety of issues.
Clyde knows as I do, that if a person is born into this world, and does not make it a better place to live than he found it, it is like he never lived at all.
GOD BLESS YOU ALWAYS.

Edward M. McIntyre
Former Richmond County Commissioner, former mayor of Augusta

Best wishes in your future endeavors. Georgia readers will greatly miss the work of one of our state's most gifted and humorous political cartoonists.

Guy W. Millner
Former and present Ga. gubernatorial candidate, former senatorial candidate

An old high school buddy (Cliff Baldowski) had a very successful career as an editorial cartoonist in Augusta and Atlanta. I asked him what the primary qualifications were for such a career.
Number one, he said, is arrogance. Number two is to have a few sadistic genes. And number three is a modest drawing talent.
Clyde Wells was certainly overqualified for his long years of writing and drawing hundreds of amusing and meaningful cartoons.
I remember the Tammany boss in New York who was quoted as saying "write whatever you want — my supporters can't read — but stop the damn pictures."
Like other office holders, I usually hated Clyde's cartoons when I was the target — but liked most of those with a different target. This feeling is general among those who have felt his sting and tells us something about his effectiveness.
I do wish him the best with this new and hopefully last book. Retirement can be wonderful and I hope his is as enjoyable as mine.

Lewis A. Newman
Former mayor of Augusta

The power of political cartoons was probably best explained by the legendary "Boss Tweed," New York's political chieftain of the 1870s and 1880s, who was the special target of the great 19th century cartoonist Thomas Nast.

Long an object of scorn among New York's many political journalists, Tweed said, "I don't care how many newspaper editorials they write against me, because most of my constituents can't read. But we have to do something to stop these pictures."

Tweed later fled the country with prosecutors in hot pursuit and was eventually captured in Spain by a policeman who recognized his face from a Nast cartoon.

I don't know of Clyde Wells single-handedly driving any rascals from office, but he has made both rascals and statesmen laugh uncomfortably over the years.

For readers of *The Augusta Chronicle*, Clyde has made the dry newsprint of political events come alive with vivid portraits of both sinners and saints.

And for those who have served in public office, Clyde has performed a uniquely valuable service that has contributed to our stewardship: He's kept us from taking ourselves too seriously.

Sam Nunn
Former United States senator, D-Ga.

As one who, from time to time, was "touched up" by your often pointed and sometimes painful pen, I am reminded of the story told about the man who had been tarred and feathered and was being ridden out of town on a rail who said, "You know, if it were not for the honor of this, I would just as soon have walked".

In public life today it seems to me that there is a shortage of good humor and an overabundance of meanness. Most of the time your cartoons were an effort to make the people involved appear as clowns rather than criminals and I really think that it is more helpful and effective in the long run. Anyone who goes into public life has to develop a thick skin, but no matter how tough you are, it hurts when your grandchildren are made to cry over some of the mean personal things that are said and printed in the newspaper.

Congratulations on your successful career and best wishes in your time of retirement.

Mike Padgett
Former Georgia state representative

In one of the most controversial decisions ever made, the citizens of Augusta and Richmond County voted to consolidate both governments effective January 1, 1996. As a former Richmond County commissioner, former chairman of the Richmond County Commissioners, and the first mayor of Augusta-Richmond County, I knew I had arrived on the political scene when I became the target of Clyde Wells' political cartoons. It was an indescribable experience to open *The Augusta Chronicle* and see my image in caricature form in his cartoon for all the readers to see. I have continued to be one of the "features" of Clyde Wells' cartoons and his intended message is never lost.

Clyde has been able to accomplish what others could never master — the ability to criticize public officials and intermix a good dose of Southern humor. Now, when I open the paper and see myself transferred from Clyde's drawing board to the editorial page, I cannot wait to call my friends and ask them if they have seen what "Clyde" did to me today.

He is a man of infinite talent who has been gracious enough to not leave the Augusta community for a bigger audience but to continuously give the readers in the Augusta-Richmond County area the pleasure of being able to enjoy his art.

I consider Clyde to be one of my best friends, and I will, without a doubt, miss him and the expectation of seeming me in boxer shorts with little pigs printed on them. I am truly sorry to see him retire, and if it meant I would have to see my image in his cartoons again, I would welcome him back without hesitation.

Good luck and God bless.

Larry E. Sconyers
Mayor of Augusta

I'm honored that, after some 17 years now, you remembered how awful you drew my face! Each time I saw my caricature featured in your space I had to run and look in the mirror to make sure I didn't really look that bad. However, you were most gracious in making me one of the good guys. Of this I was most thankful! The only humor I found in the long four years I served as a Richmond County commissioner was your wonderful cartoons.

Your editorial cartoons were always my most favorite part of the newspaper. You have such a wonderful knack for being right on target, telling so much in a small space about how it really is. Between you and Margaret Twiggs, I could keep up with the pulse of politics in and around us. It was quite an enlightening time.

You have such a talent and I truly feel the Augusta area has been quite fortunate to have had you there all these years. I for one hate to see you retire but certainly wish the best for you in your next endeavor.

Barbara Mulherin Scott
Former Richmond County Commissioner

I suppose a lot of state and local officials feel they can relax a little now that Clyde Wells has retired. That's just one of many reasons I'm sad to see this talented man call it a day, at least as far as his work at *The Augusta Chronicle*. Over the years, Clyde's editorial cartoons probably were more effective than any other form of journalism at keeping many elected officials and other leaders in line, or at least from straying too far over it. Politicians held their breath every time they turned to one of Clyde's cartoons for fear he had made them the target of his biting wit on that particular day. You could almost hear the sighs of relief from those who found no caricatures of themselves, as well as the muffled curses of those who did.

I know what I'm talking about because for a few years in the late '70s and early '80s, I was one of the politicians holding his breath. Fortunately, Clyde wasn't too hard on me during my tenure on the Richmond County Commission, but I'd like to think that if he had been, I still would have appreciated the fact he used his considerable skills to serve the public as an effective government watchdog. But even when his subjects weren't political, Clyde always hit the mark. Who could forget his image of the space shuttle Challenger entering eternal rest in the outstretched hands of God?

Clyde left big shoes to fill, but I can't imagine that anybody ever will. I wish him the happiest of retirements, and I thank him for allowing me to breathe all those sighs of relief.

Harold C. Smith
Former Richmond County Commissioner

I was overwhelmingly honored at your request for my contribution to your third book, a compilation of almost twenty-seven years of editorial cartoons. Thank you — I think!

It certainly is delightful now for me to browse over the editorial page with a sigh of emotional relief. This is unquestionably due to the fact that I have retired from the educational arena. But the truth of the matter is that I generally did appreciate your timely creative artistic genius even while I was in a position of vulnerability to your "satiric musings."

Obviously, I could not agree with all of your artistic renditions, especially those that were pertaining to my administrative tenure. How in the world could you have been so misguided?! (A humble attempt of levity?)

Even though I did receive some of your professional attention on the editorial page, I generally found your cartoons to be germane to many issues. I know that you realized that some of your cartoons had negative ramifications for many individuals. This indeed was an awesome moralistic aspect of your position that you took very seriously.

All in all, I seriously did find you to be a man of integrity, honesty, professionalism, tenacity, wit, and courage. It is these exact qualities that have made our friendship so enjoyable over the years.

I wish you a long, healthy and rewarding future. By the way, do you recall the luncheon we had with the "famous editorial writer" early in my superintendency? You said that you were there (much to my surprise) to study my physical features for the cartoons that were sure to follow. My family members and I have agreed that your caricatures were not up to your usual high professional standards. (I had to inject that!)

I really enjoy being without a job. You will too! Enjoy life.

John P. Strelec
Former Richmond County School Superintendent

Throughout the ages, humor has been a great tonic for mankind. It gives a different and unique perspective on the human condition. Augusta has been fortunate to have had Clyde Wells' brand of humor over the years. He has entertained as well as enlightened the public, most at the expense of elected officials like me. I have been the target of his cartoons for many years and can say that Clyde has never used his great talent to denigrate or intentionally harm anyone. He has been very successful at tickling our funny bones with his cartoons. He gave me many chuckles and much publicity over the years, and indeed, still does.

I wish him well and a long life.

Harrell Tiller
Former Richmond County Commissioner

The ability to capture in a caricature the core of knotty issues and the incongruities of public life is a talent possessed by very few. Clyde Wells is the most gifted that I have known.

An editorial cartoon, like a written editorial, is an expression of one's opinion, not an unbiased, unslanted statement of fact. It is often a half truth or a truth and a half. However, all public figures are equally subject to Mr. Wells' satire, regardless of political party. Inconsistencies of opinion which even the occasional reader observes in written editorials are not found in Mr. Wells' cartooning.

Mr. Wells not only documented our evolving local history in his unique style, he flavored it, and by osmosis over a period of three decades became a part of it himself. He has now acted on his long contemplated retirement as editorial cartoonist for *The Augusta Chronicle* — he will be missed.

Tom Tinley
Former Richmond County Commissioner

I greet the news of your impending retirement with mixed emotions. While it is sad that one so talented will no longer be exposed to the community, it is with great joy that I contemplate the positive impact your retirement will have on race relations in this community. Your insensitivity has shone as brightly as the morning sun rising over the Savannah. Mr. Wells, your place in Augusta editorial history is firmly established as a member of the right-wing, intolerant, editorial duo which included the late Margaret Twiggs.

You are, no doubt, proud that your Sambo-inspired characterizations are in the same psychological vein as D.W. Griffith's *Birth of a Nation* (1915) and Thomas Dixon's *The Clansman* (1905). They, too, were great artists.

By the way, enjoy your retirement. I do not expect to be paid for this submission. Therefore, I suggest you donate the complimentary copy of your new book to the Christian Coalition, better yet the Skin Heads.

Charles W. Walker

Georgia senate Majority Leader, District 22

I began serving as sheriff of Richmond County in 1984 and, to this day, I am reminded of the humor and serious pen power of cartoonist Clyde Wells. His cartoons over many years contributed to community respect for how he views complex issues with a stroke of the pen. Several times, in fact, I have been on the receiving end of the pen only to become another victim "bitten," and, in most cases, deserved it.

Events in our community and in our nation have surrendered to pen on pad with Clyde at the controls. Clyde can bring humor, anger or tears to the best of us with his abilities. He has become a popular cartoonist and friend to many in Augusta while achieving status as one of the best editorial cartoonists in the country.

I'm sure this book representing a lifetime of the best of Clyde will be forever remembered as his masterpiece. The collections cover much territory and hopefully Clyde, with pen in hand, will continue to entertain us during his golden years. May I say as you exit the cartoonist arena where you have shined so well: "Wells done."

Charlie Webster

Richmond County Sheriff

To borrow from the great poet Robert Burns – if we could "see ourselves as others see us!" To be seen from Clyde Wells' perspective can be exhilarating or humbling.

Too often, elected officials become so overwhelmed with themselves and their importance that it takes a humbling reminder from Clyde Wells to bring us down to the size of the fallible human beings that we are. Clyde's irreverence for politics and politicians is perfectly balanced by his reverence for those events involving individuals who have given their all to improve the world.

Through the years it has been my pleasure to have observed Clyde Wells, and on occasion, to have been observed by him. In the future I hope Clyde will be compelled to continue sharing his observations of those events that need the interpretation only he can bring.

Inez Wylds

Former Augusta city council member

Those invitees who chose not to respond

James Beck
Former Augusta Chief of Police, former Richmond County Sheriff

Freddy Handy
Richmond County Commissioner

Henry Brigham
Richmond County Commissioner

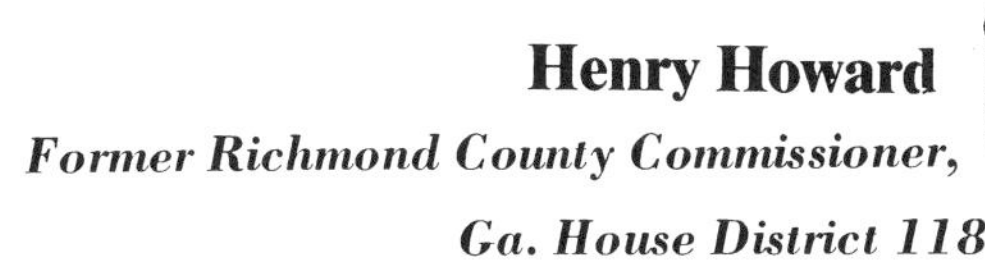

Henry Howard
Former Richmond County Commissioner, Ga. House District 118

James Brown
Entertainer

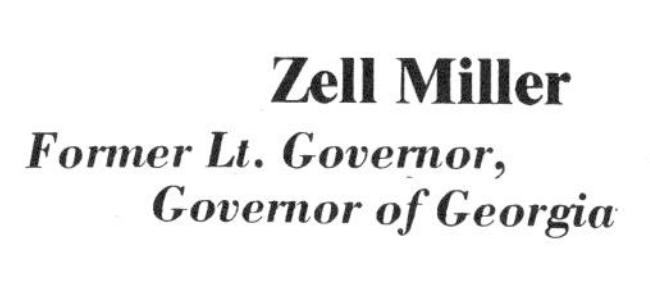

Zell Miller
Former Lt. Governor, Governor of Georgia

Hobson Chavous
Former Richmond County Commissioner

Tom Murphy
Speaker of the Georgia House of Representatives

Jack Connell
Speaker Pro Tempore of the House, District 115

Moses Todd
Richmond County Commissioner

Those invitees for whom no mailing address could be found

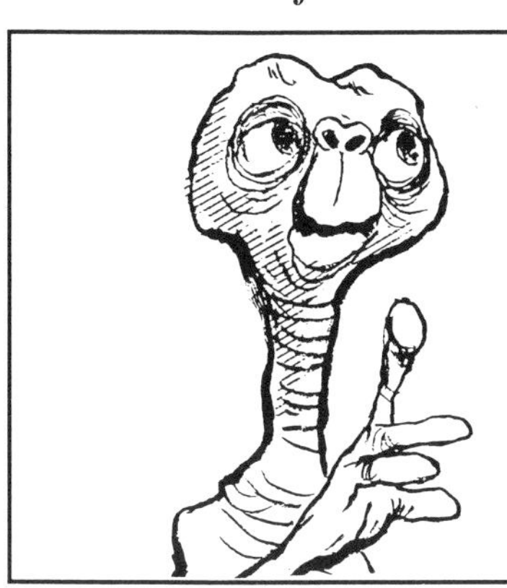

E.T.

Yoda

Those who would have been invited and who would have responded

IN MEMORIAM

Jesse Carroll
1924-1991
Richmond County Commissioner

Robert C. (Bobby) Daniel, Jr.
1943-1993
Richmond County Attorney

Otis Hensley
1935-1994
Columbia County Sheriff

... To Uphold and Defend ... for Life! ...'

OFFICER CANDIDATE SCHOOL

CALLEY

WELLS

4-1-71

First cartoon

Lt. Calley is found guilty for his role in the My Lai massacre. The Augusta Chronicle opposes his sentence of life imprisonment. (Note the date...April Fool's Day. Also the general has his LEFT hand raised in the swearing-in ceremony. Not an auspicious start.)

Second cartoon – The first of many Masters related cartoons and drawings. Not a very good rendition. I don't think I would have hired me as a cartoonist.

An early, rather innocuous effort aimed at the county commission, from left, Woo, Clifford, Neal, McIntyre, and Troutman.

Gov. Jimmy Carter cleans up Long County's speed traps.

The reason a cartoonist was hired by the Chronicle – to help in passing a referendum consolidating the governments of Augusta and Richmond County.

In 1968, it was Spiro Who? Spiro Agnew returns the favor on George McGovern's choice of Sen. Thomas Eagleton as his running mate. Previous treatment for mental problems force Eagleton to step aside and Kennedy-in-law Sargent Shriver joins George on his ill-fated quest for the presidency.

Nixon mines Haiphong harbor and hopes for the best.

Richard Milhous Nixon wins by a landslide, losing only Massachusetts and the District of Columbia.

Jimmy Carter succeeded Lester Maddox as governor of Georgia in January 1971. Prohibited by law from succeeding himself, Maddox easily won election as lieutenant governor. As presiding officer of the Senate, the lieutenant governor, along with the speaker of the House, affected the movement of legislation through their respective chambers. Needless to say, cooperation between them and the governor facilitated the passage of legislation. The Carter-Maddox political feud became legendary. Its origins are obscure but it quickly deteriorated into an intense personal dislike to the extent that during the next four years, the business of government was on occasion adversely affected. One of their early battles centered around state reapportionment with each determined to reward friends and punish enemies.

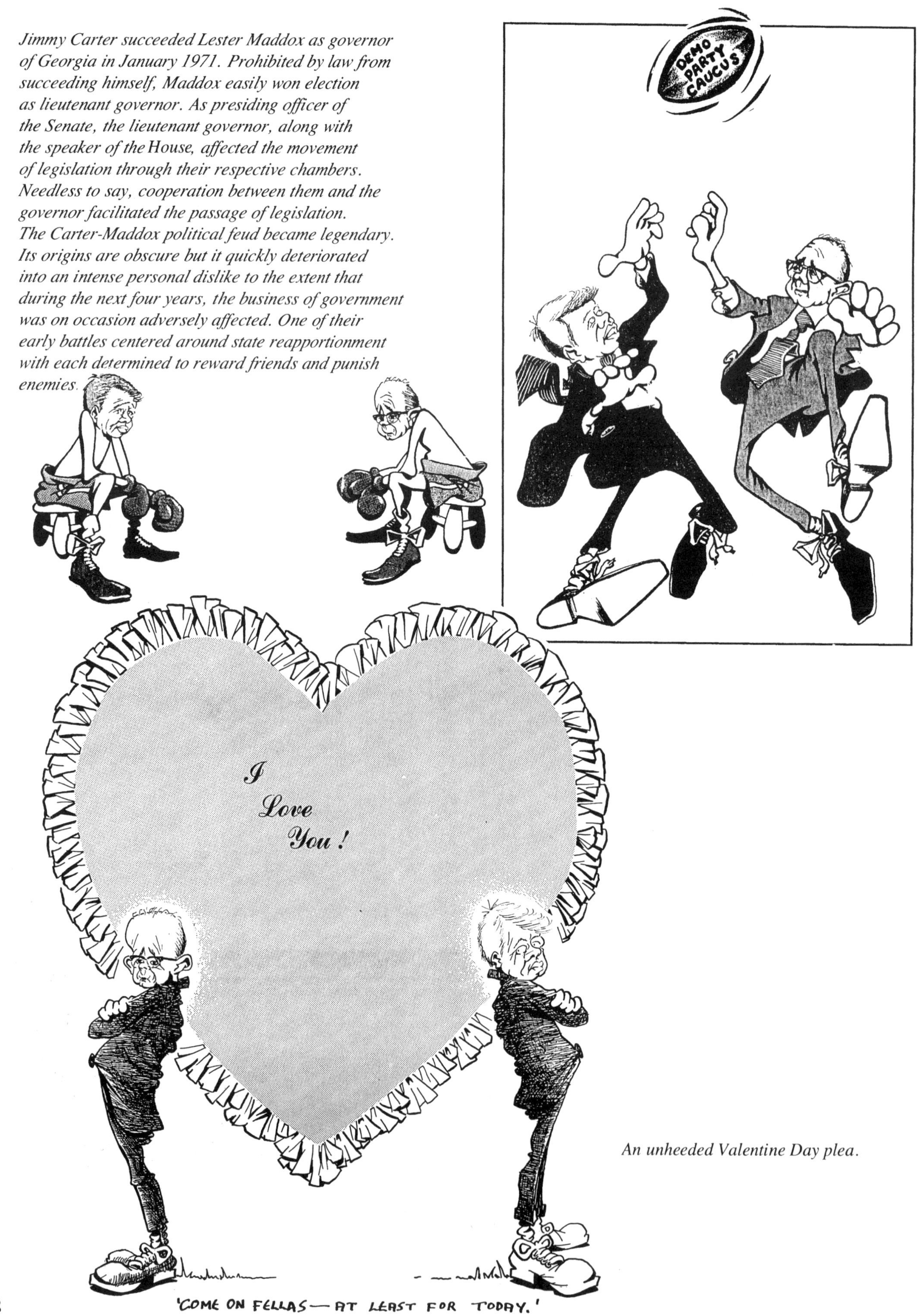
DEMO PARTY CAUCUS
I Love You!
'COME ON FELLAS—AT LEAST FOR TODAY.'

An unheeded Valentine Day plea.

Carter and the General Assembly agree to reverse their legislative roles in his ambitions to reorganize Georgia's state government. He succeeded on a promise of more efficiency and economy. A promise that did not materialize.

At the 1972 Democratic Convention in Miami Beach, Jimmy fails to stop the George McGovern nomination. Others would fail to stop Jimmy in 1976.

Georgia's power trio – Lester, Jimmy and Herman.

Lester's new springtime look included a hairpiece, which he mercifully discarded after a few weeks. That it added to the Maddox 'mystique' was questionable.

Knowing Lester's ego, was there ever any doubt which way he would jump? It was generally conceded at the time that he could easily win either seat.

LBJ 1908-1973

Lyndon Baines Johnson,
36th president, is dead.

FBI chief J. Edgar Hoover dies on May 2, 1972.

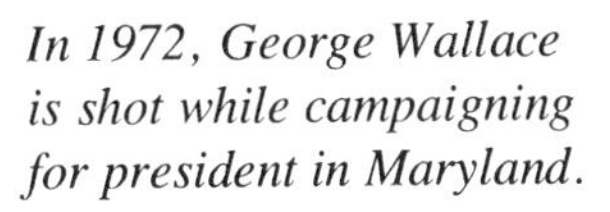

In 1972, George Wallace is shot while campaigning for president in Maryland.

Three time Masters Champions

Sam Snead
1949-52-54

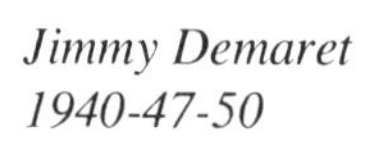

Jimmy Demaret
1940-47-50

State Rep. Sam Nunn from Perry was the winner in a crowded primary field for the Democratic Senate nomination. In his campaign against Republican Fletcher Thompson, he assumes a heavy burden in George McGovern, the ultra-liberal Democratic presidential nominee.

Sen. Richard Russell's death in 1971 spawned a bevy of contenders in 1972. Former governor Carl Sanders mulls a run, but decides against it. Perhaps his failed gubernatorial race against Jimmy Carter two years earlier influenced his decision.

Lester's endorsement is a much sought-after prize in campaign '72.

On the evening of June 17, 1972, a break-in of Democratic National headquarters, located in the Watergate complex, resulted in the arrests of seven people. Nine months later it seemed the whole affair would quietly blow away. Then, on March 23, 1973, one of the seven conspirators, James McCord, in a letter to Judge John Sirica, told of pressures on the seven to keep silent. It became apparent that the White House was involved. A Select Senate Committee, chaired by Sen. Sam Ervin of North Carolina, was impaneled to investigate. The trail led to the Oval Office and it became obvious that there were questions that only Nixon could answer. He was a no-show.

During the Senate Watergate Committee hearings, it was learned that tape recordings of Oval Office conversations existed. Nixon refused to release them to the Committee, invoking the doctrine of executive privilege. Eventually, the Supreme Court would order him to turn over the tapes relating to Watergate discussions. His back was finally to the wall.

'Chairman Rodino, please...yes...Hello, Peter! About your (expletive) disenchantment with my (unintelligible) transcripts. My (irrelevant) opinion is that you are (inaudible) and, futhermore, (expletive) (unintelligible) and also (inaudible) (expletive) (irrelevent)...'

Milhous responds to House Judiciary Committee Chairman Peter Rodino's disenchantment with the transcripts of the White House tapes. Among other bits of pertinent information, the 'editing' process removed some rather salty language by our chief executive and friends.

One moment, Rev. Graham--I'll see if he's in..!"

Good friend, the Rev. Billy Graham, stops by to discuss Milhous' expletives.

On August 5, President Nixon was forced to release White House tape transcripts that proved he had conspired to obstruct justice in the Watergate investigations. The House Judiciary Committee had already voted three articles of impeachment — obstructing justice, abuse of presidential power, and subversion of constitutional government. On August 8, 1974, Richard M. Nixon became the first President of the United States to resign from office.

Gerald Ford becomes the nation's 38th president.

Sen. Hubert Humphrey

Vice President Nelson Rockefeller

Ford pardons Nixon. It would prove fatal to his presidential hopes in the 1976 campaign against Jimmy Carter.

Adolph, Milhouse and Richmond County Sheriff Bill Anderson. Would they lie to us? Yes.

Fuel shortages — the energy crisis is upon us.

A record fourteen inches of snow fell during the great 'Blizzard of '73.'

CHIEF
JAMES G. BECK
SHERIFF
WM. A. ANDERSON

As feuds go, the Beck-Anderson match-up ranked right down there with Jimmy and Lester's.

Mayor Lewis A. (Pop) Newman, referring to Sheriff William A. Anderson as Wyatt Earp, complained that city residents were not getting their tax-money's worth. Their county tax bill supported a sheriff's department that patrolled mainly the unincorporated areas of Richmond County, leaving the city to the Augusta Police Department. The mayor's object was to halt increased funding for the sheriff's department. Wyatt, hoping to cut the mayor off at the pass, countered by moving his patrols into the city. It was not recorded as to whether city residents felt any safer.

'Wyatt Earp, Wyatt Earp,
Brave, courageous and bold.
Long live his fame
and long live his glory,
and long may his story be told!'
AUGUSTA GA. CITY LIMITS
SOMEBODY CALL A COP!
APOLOGIES TO OLIPHANT
WEISS
SUNDAY CHRONICLE-HERALD

Sheriff Anderson's 'early release' program gets out of hand.

Sheriff Anderson sends Valentine Day greetings to three 'cityside' state representatives following their refusal to endorse a request for additional deputies.

To destroy a work of man's creative beauty is to bruise the soul of all those who ever looked upon it.
LOT
FOR SALE
ZONED
FOR BUSINESS
WELLS
SUNDAY CHRONICLE-HERALD

The grand and historic Sacred Heart church has a date with the wrecker's ball. It would be saved by the benevolence of Mr. Peter Knox, Jr. It is now the Sacred Heart Cultural Center.

Some local partisan political rhetoric with a bicentennial flair.

Another city-county consolidation bill is before the county delegation. Rep. Jack Connell is an early holdout. Reason was to prevail, however, and the bill was presented for local voters' approval. It failed. Two similar bills, calling for the consolidation of Augusta and Richmond County governments, had also previously failed to pass.

The county delegation finds it difficult to keep on truckin'.

The great 'Blizzard of '79'.

Richmond County built a brand new courthouse once and look what happened to them.

Port Augusta, a dream that would never be realized, gets a shallow send-off from the Corps of Engineers.

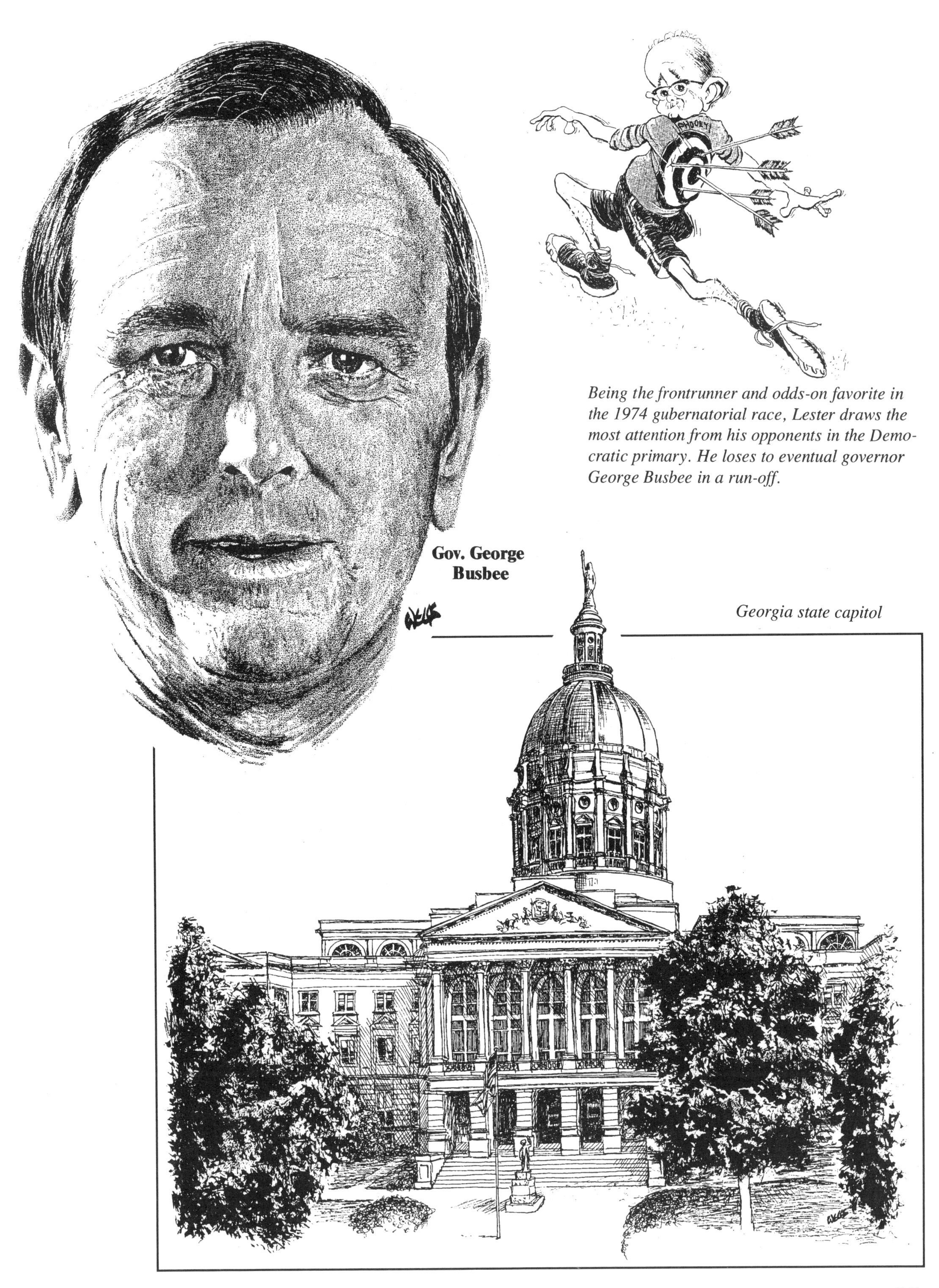

Being the frontrunner and odds-on favorite in the 1974 gubernatorial race, Lester draws the most attention from his opponents in the Democratic primary. He loses to eventual governor George Busbee in a run-off.

Gov. George Busbee

Georgia state capitol

The dreams of Bobby Jones and Clifford Roberts gave birth to the Augusta National Golf Club and, subsequently, to the Masters Tournament.

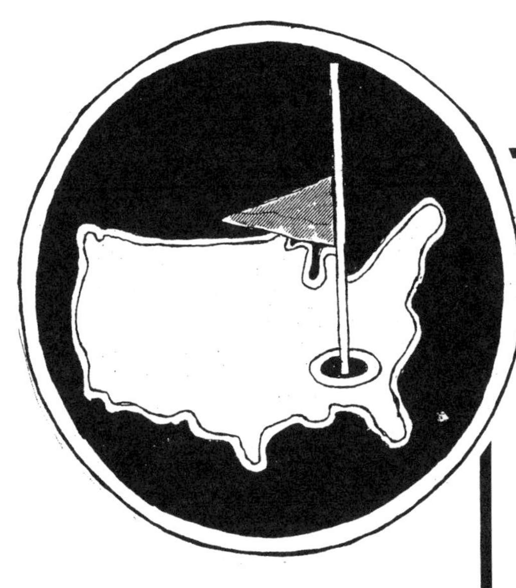

Clifford Roberts
1894-1977

The light at the end of all tunnels!

For too many years and too many lives, America's leadership kept seeing the light at the end of the tunnel in the Vietnam War. In April 1975, the war ended. There was no light—only humiliation for the United States. Nearly 57,000 lives lost, many more thousands maimed and crippled, and $150 billion spent in a losing war with a small, third-rate country. Christians all over America took solace on this Easter Sunday in recognizing the real light at the end of all life's tunnels.

A good man, the president of Paine College, passes away.

Atlanta Brave Henry Aaron hits home run number 715, breaking Babe Ruth's career record. His final total would be 755.

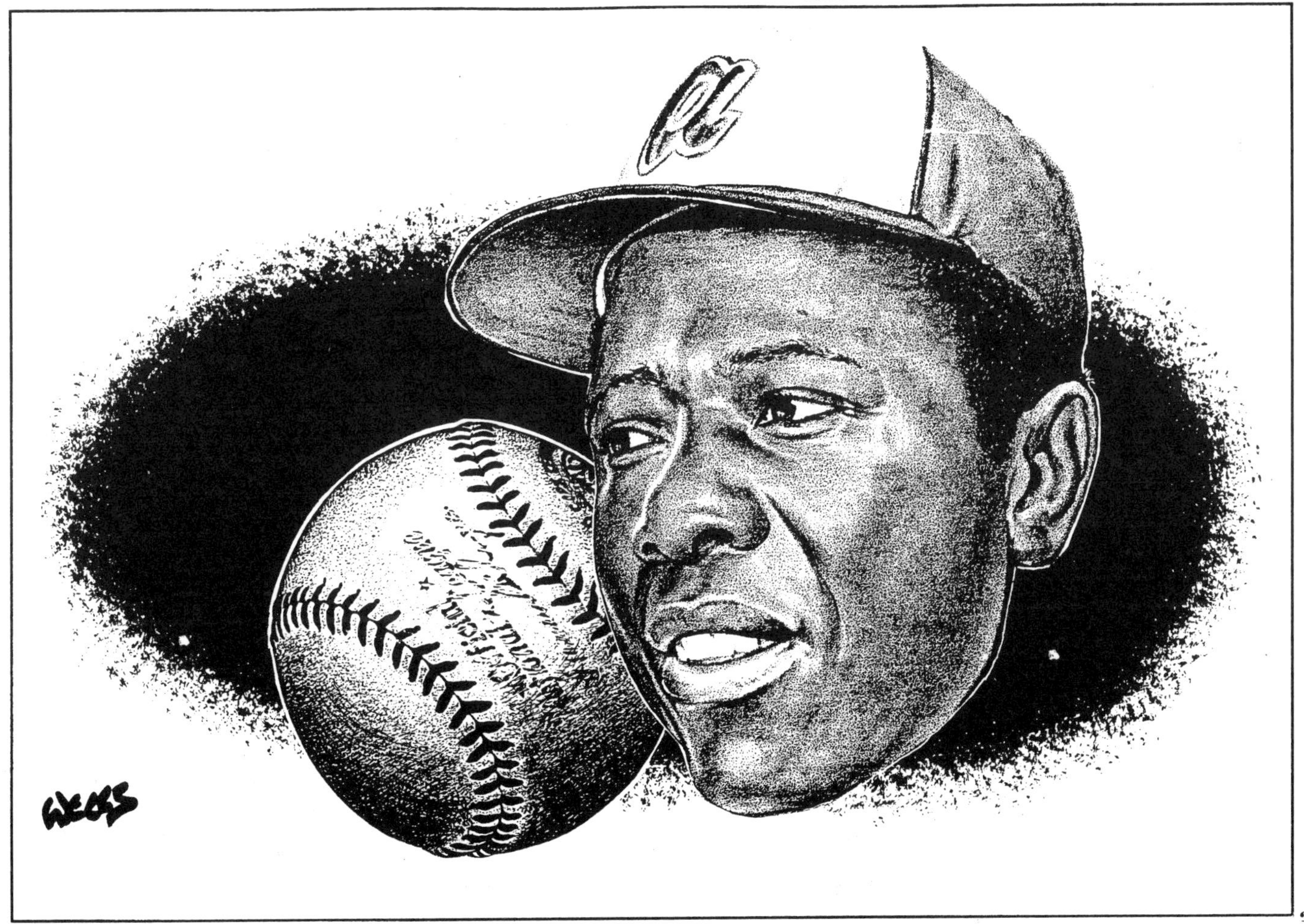

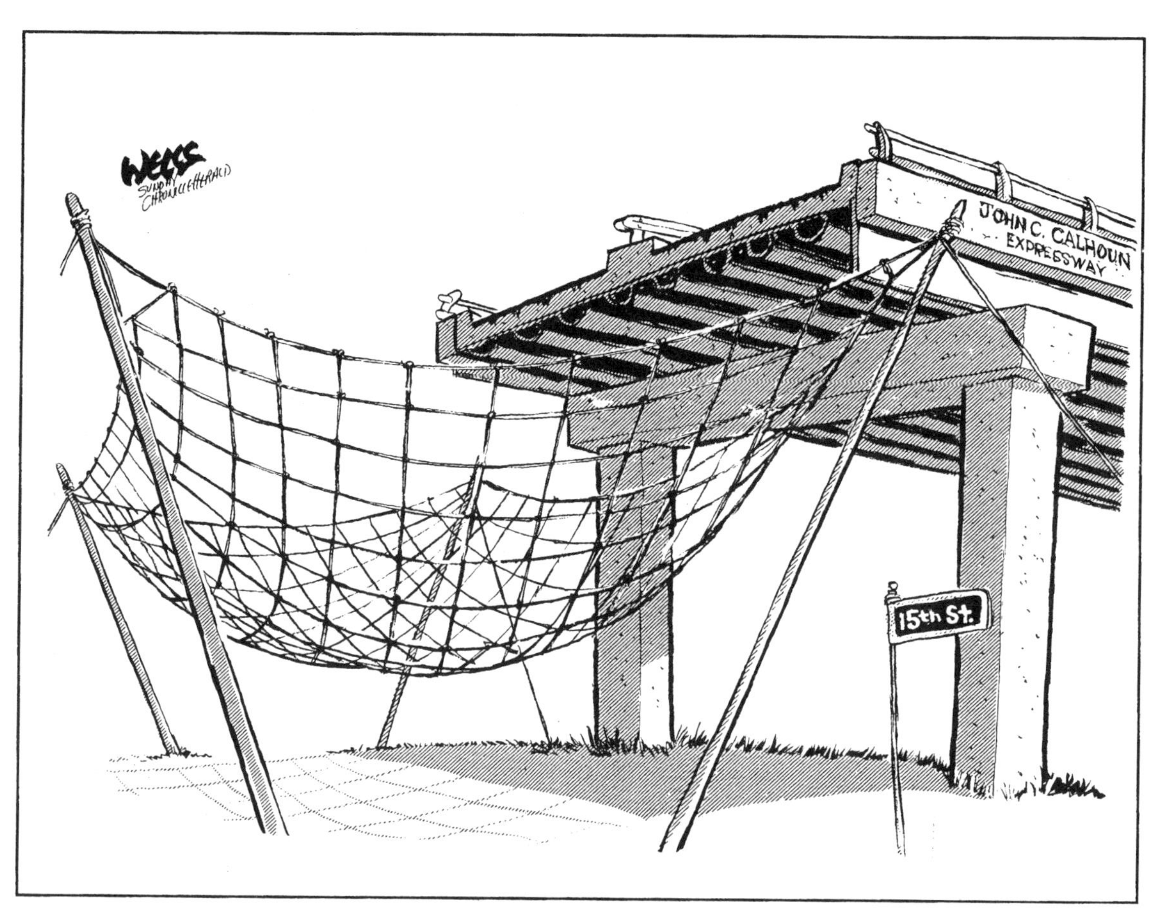

A 1.8 mile stretch of expressway, connecting Lake Olmstead and Sears department store, ends abruptly at 15th Street. A few months later it is opened to the driving public.

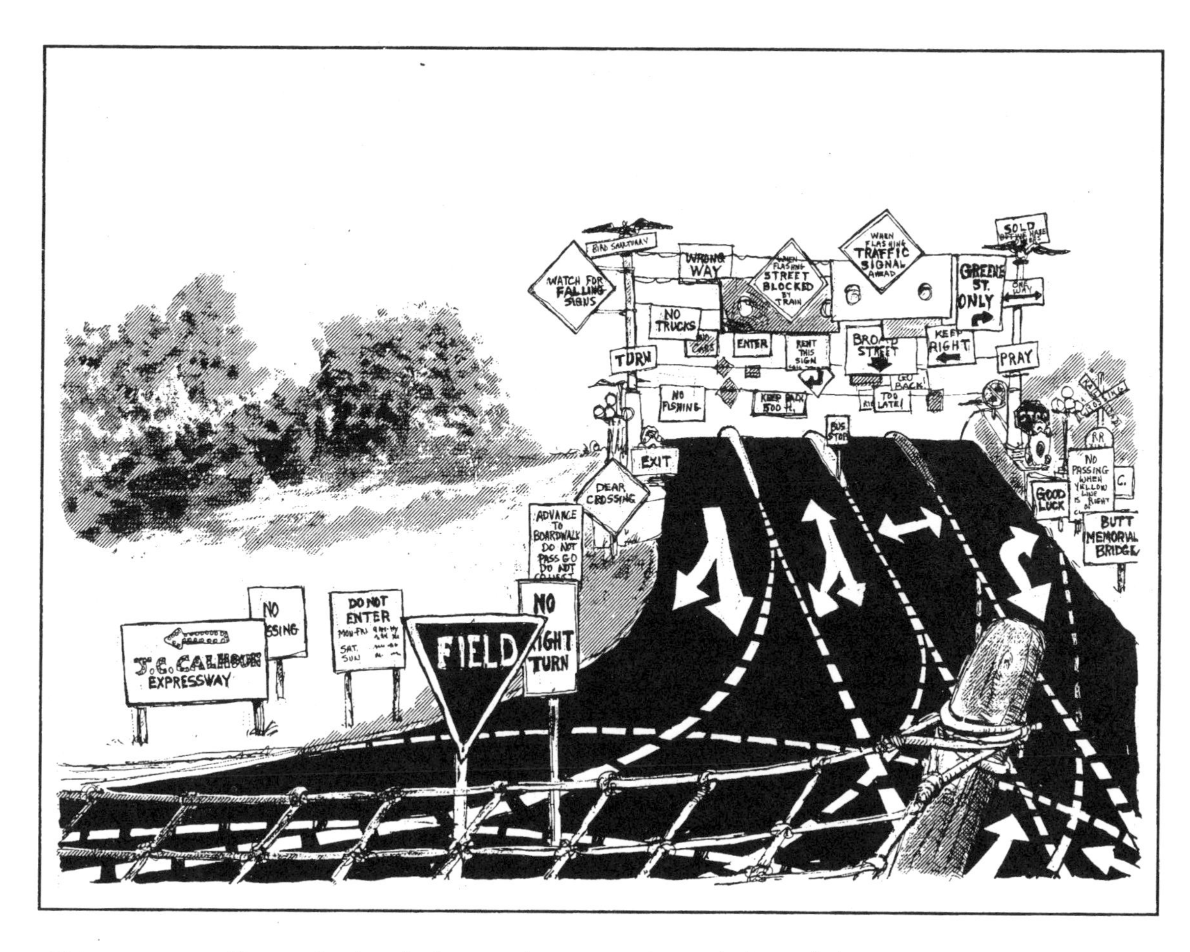

This causes a traffic overload at the intersection, prompting a plethora of signs and signals at the Butt Memorial Bridge hump. In 1984, nine years later, the expressway is extended a few hundred yards further to the Greyhound bus station.

Strom & Nancy have their fourth young 'un. Strong measures are called for.

Support your local hoax. Questions (and answers) arose as to the authenticity of Augusta's historic MacKay House.

Courtroom sketch — Criminal Court, McCormick, South Carolina

From left, Judge Grimball hands down life sentences to James and David Morrison, convicted of murdering three soldiers at Clarks Hill. Attorneys Frank Harrison and Julius Baggett look on.

RICHMOND COUNTY ATTORNEY ROBERT C. DANIEL AND FRIEND

I HAVE RECOMMENDED TO THE COUNTY COMMISSION THAT THE TAPES OF THEIR JULY 17 MEETING, OWING TO PENDING LEGAL ACTION IN MATTERS DISCUSSED RE: THE PUBLIC'S BUSINESS, SHOULD NOT BE HEARD BY THE CITIZENS OF RICHMOND COUNTY.

LOTSA LUCK!

You don't need the Supreme Court to tell you.
The citizens of Richmond County heard the tapes.

1976 dawns with great promise. The nation's 200th birthday and a presidential election year of special interest to Georgians. Jimmy Carter is making a serious challenge for the Democratic presidential nomination. Meanwhile, President Ford is having problems holding his No. 1 position in the Republican Party.

Panama agitates for control of the Panama Canal. The controversy would culminate in aborting the treaty that gave control of the Canal in perpetuity to the United States. President Jimmy Carter would sign a treaty two years later giving Panama, in stages, complete control by 1999.

Gov. Carter announces his candidacy for the presidency in October 1974. The nomination process, having moved from the back rooms to open primaries, would enable a southern governor to win the nomination.

Jimmy's admission of occasional lustful urges in a Playboy interview creates consternation in the Carter camp.

Jimmy's campaign stature grows.

The Georgia General Assembly convenes and our crack county delegation, with our destinies securely in tow, heads for Atlanta and returns, the city and county intact.

Above from left: Reps. R.A. Dent, Mike Padgett, Jack Connell, Don Cheeks, Bill Jackson (Columbia County), Sens. Jimmy Lester and Tom Allgood and Rep. Danny Daniel and the lone Republican, Rep. David Swann.

The outsider will think this is a fabricated situation. It isn't. The only deviation from fact is, in real life, the raspberry solution was in a liquid state, the easier to mix with the resident content.

Would you believe it? The unlimited terms proposal includes Council members, too.

In 1972, Pop Newman won his first term as mayor, largely on the promise to rid downtown Augusta of its many rail crossings. Though the mayor worked and prayed hard for rail removal, most of the tracks are still there. It has been the duty of a public-spirited press to remind him of this fact periodically.

Aid from Washington was a long time coming.

Pop runs a wide-awake campaign.

Pop gets his re-election campaign on track.

Carter wins...

...and the Southern influence would soon be felt in Washington.

Don't get mad. Get even.

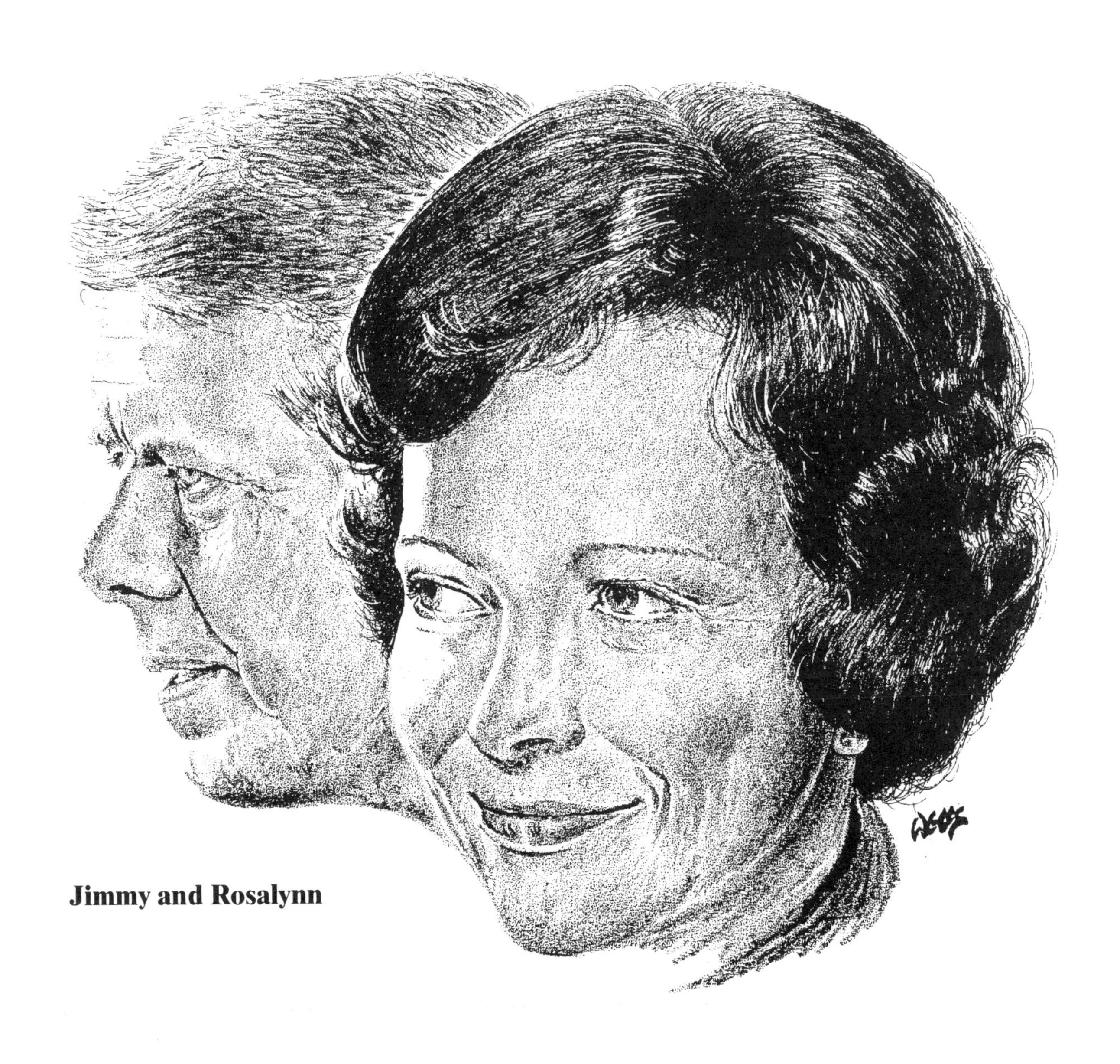

Jimmy and Rosalynn

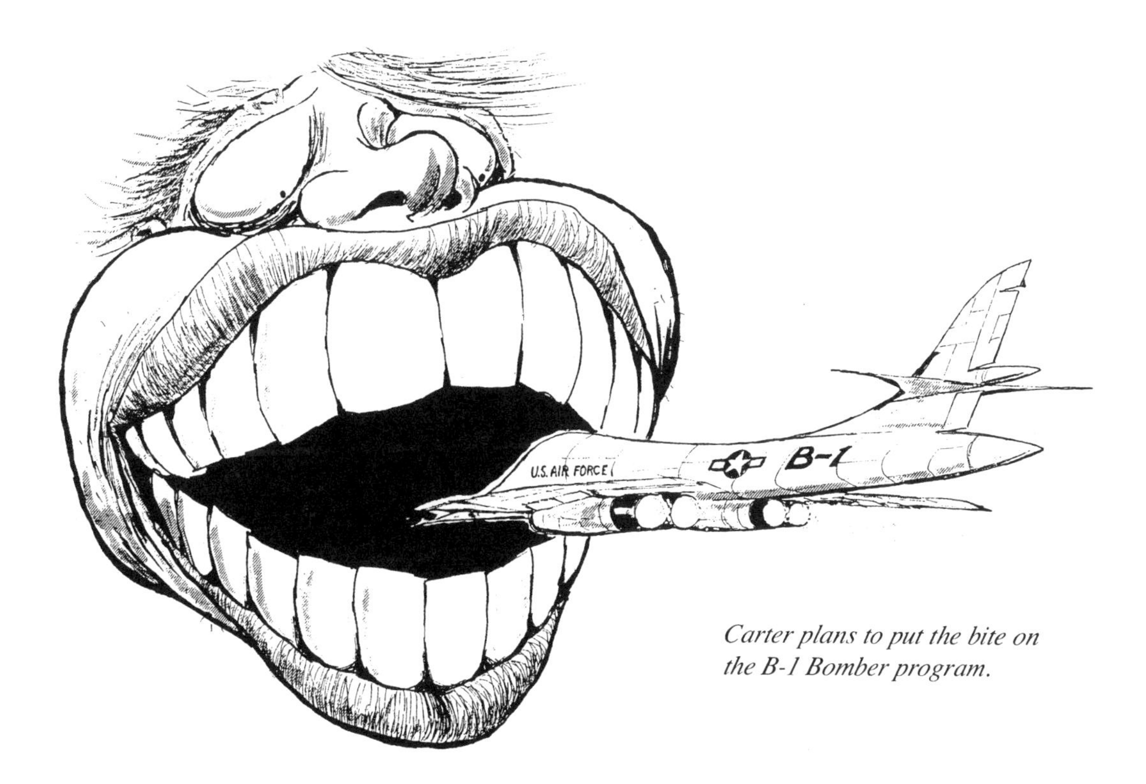

Carter plans to put the bite on the B-1 Bomber program.

Carter nominates old Georgia pal Bert Lance for director of the Office of Management and Budget. Serious improprieties in Lance's past banking practices surface during Senate Governmental Affairs Committee hearings. Carter vows support and praises Lance.

The Kremlin reacts to Carter's human rights campaign by harassing, exiling and jailing Soviet dissidents.

In a little under three years as UN ambassador,
Andrew Young brings a new meaning to the term FAUX PAS.

Jimmy and his foreign policy team leave a lot to be desired.

Two words describe the administration's leadership and direction in foreign policy: Abundant and varied.

Our NATO allies feel let down when Carter cancels the neutron bomb program.

ADM. ECONOMIC ADVISORS

WHY, AS A MATTER OF FACT, WE ARE LOST. HOW DID YOU KNOW?

The Federal Reserve Board increases interest rates to combat double-digit inflation. Unemployment is almost 8 percent. The deficit, forecast to be $15 billion, climbs to a shortfall of $60 billion. Productivity declines. 1980 was not Jimmy's year.

On November 4, 1979, 52 Americans are taken hostage by Iranian 'students' and held in the American embassy in Tehran. Sanctioned by the government of Iran and its leader, the Ayatollah Khomeini, attempts to gain their release prove to be exercises in futility.

When it becomes apparent Phase I isn't working, Jimmy doesn't hesitate to bring in a hard-hitting Phase II.

A note from Billy…
"Believe me, after the last year I know what its like to be under attack."

Billy Carter

Two Soviet-built Libyan fighters are shot down after attacking two U.S. Navy F-14 jets 60 miles off the Libyan coast. (During the Carter administration, Billy Carter enjoyed a special relationship with the Libyan government.)

When entering battle, Japan's war cry is "Tora! Tora! Tora!" When foreign auto sales, led by the Japanese, reach a record 26.5 percent of the U.S. market, American auto makers react with their own.

Milhous retires to his California seaside estate, San Clemente. His two favorite reporters, Bob Woodward and Carl Bernstein of the Washington Post, who were responsible for breaking the Watergate story, collaborate on two books, one of which is made into a movie.

A good, clean cheap shot.

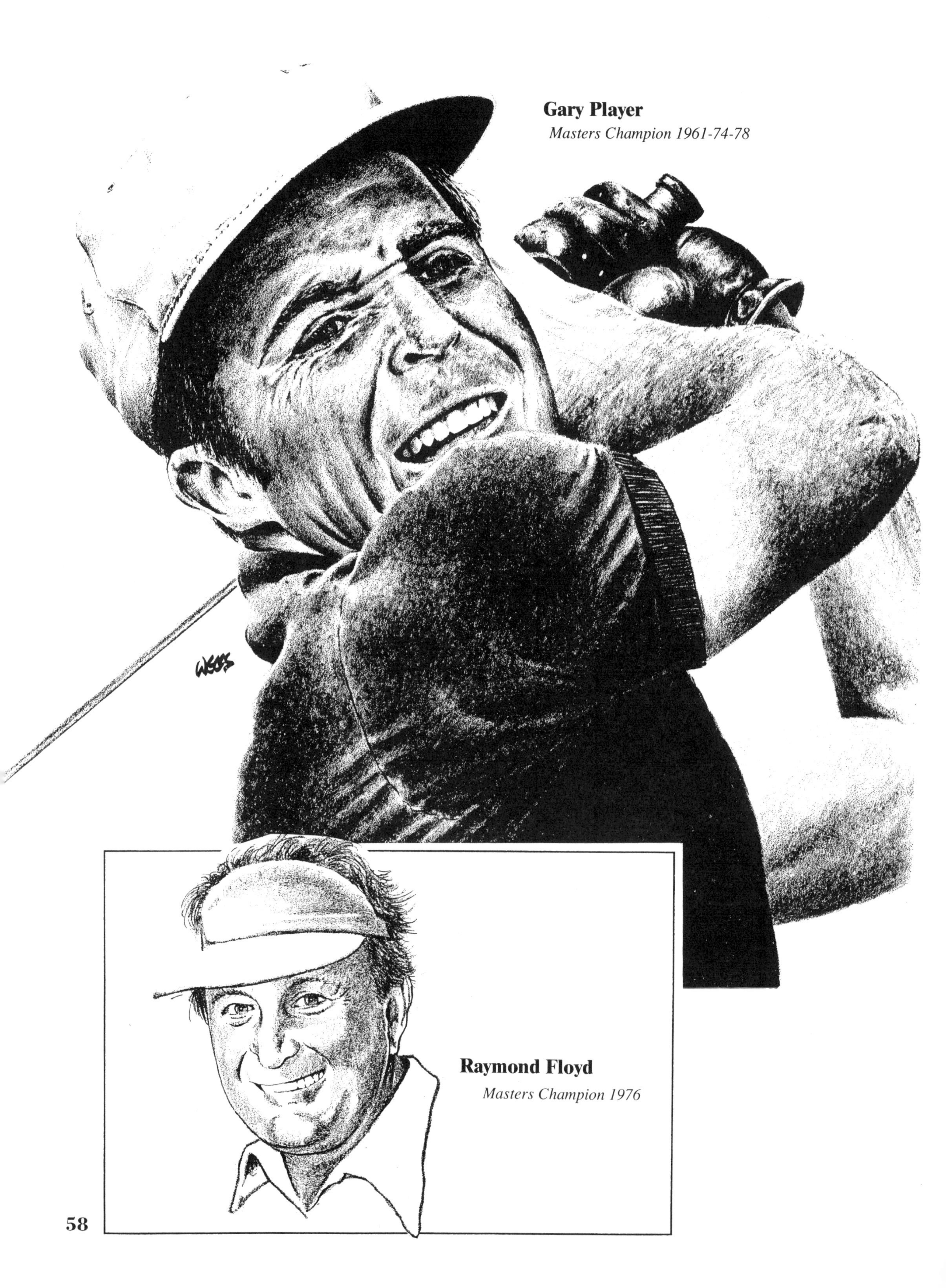

Gary Player

Masters Champion 1961-74-78

Raymond Floyd

Masters Champion 1976

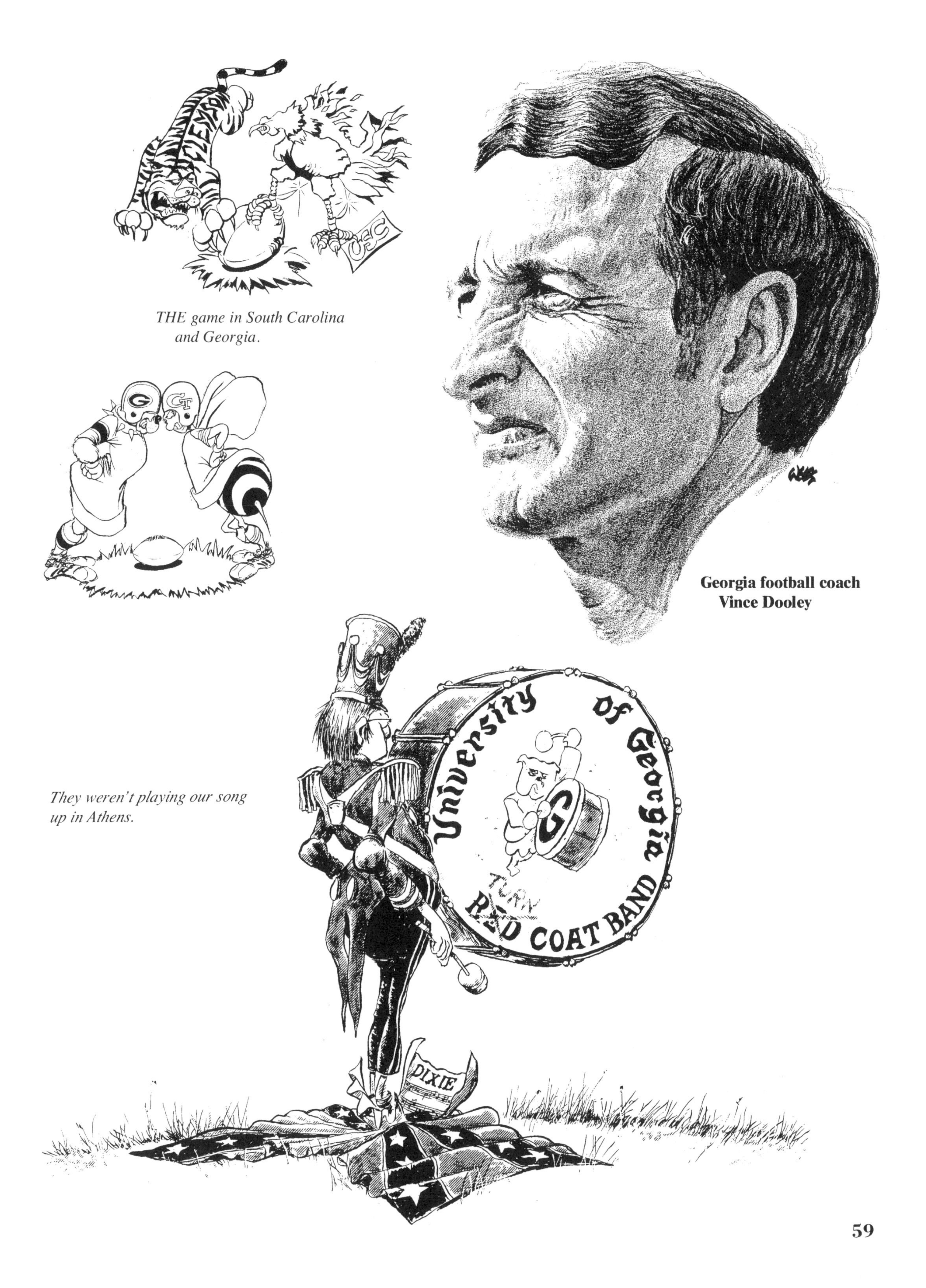

THE game in South Carolina and Georgia.

Georgia football coach Vince Dooley

They weren't playing our song up in Athens.

Introductions and explanations are in order. The Richmond County Board of Commissioners, vintage 1976, from left, John Anderson, Donald C. Neal, Chairman Edward M. McIntyre, Harrell S. Tiller and Norman Simowitz in session. Neal, McIntyre and Tiller coalesced into a loose alliance that surfaced repeatedly through 1978, the expiration of their terms.

The July 4th bicentennial calls for burying the time capsule for 100 years Can you dig it?

Suggestion of the week

It's Academy Award time and local talents are properly recognized.

Introducing two concerned citizens..er..two new county commissioners, Travis Barnes and Barbara Mulherin Scott, from left and outside of noose.

Harrell 1 is re-crowned chairman.

Correction. Neal later decided not to seek reelection. The others would have been so wise.

Neal apparently figured his "statue of limitations" was up. To his credit, he left the others one vote shy in their attempt to pack boards, commissions, etc. with friendly appointees. The terms of the three mercifully expired as 1978 faded into history.

It is revealed that some county officials are living rather high on the hog at local taxpayer's expense while visiting the Big Apple.

Lo and behold! Some city folk had stopped at Hotel Pierre at taxpayer's expense, too.

Feeling that the Augusta Police Department is not adhering quickly enough to federally-mandated affirmative action hiring guidelines, Federal Judge Anthony A. Alaimo, for all practical purposes, assumes command.

The steel framework of the new VA hospital leans a mite in the early stages of construction. A few well placed rivets and the only thing hurt is pride.

'Oops!'

A beautiful stretch of white water on the upper Savannah River is too much for the Feds. The Richard B. Russell Dam project is put into motion.

D. Douglas supports the Russell Dam project. Jimmy threatens veto of the overall water projects bill, calling it pork barrel politics.

Congressman Doug Barnard

Tom Watson
1977 Masters winner

Masters Edition cover drawing. 13th hole-Augusta National

Summer, 1978. The malls open and downtown Augusta feels deserted.

An annexation vote is in for Mayor Pop.

State Rep. Mike Padgett pays a visit to two of the new commissioners.

New commissioners, Harold Smith, Frank Albert and Bill Hiers join Barnes and Scott. In time, politics would cause a grayish tinge on the hats and flecks of rust on the halos, but all things considered, an big improvement.

BARNES
SMITH
ALBERT
SCOTT
HIERS
RICHMOND CO. BOARD OF COMMISSIONERS OFFICIAL 1979 PORTRAIT. (NOTE THAT THE COMMISSION HAS BEEN EXPANDED FROM A 3 TO A 5-PERSON BOARD.) HONORING THE TIME-HONORED ADAGE OF, 'ALWAYS GIVE A SUCKER AN EVEN BREAK', THE COMMISSION IS DEPICTED WEARING WHITE HATS & HALOS, SIGNIFYING GOODNESS, PURITY & GOVERNMENT OF, FOR & BY THE PEOPLE. THIS WILL PROBABLY CHANGE.

The ghosts of county commissioners past greet the newly appointed county administrator.

Things go from bad to worse for Jimmy. Declaring a ''malaise on the land'', he summons America's best Democratic brains to Camp David to solve the problem. After ten days, he comes down with the solution.

Jimmy meets resistance in trying to bring Egyptian President Anwar Sadat and Israeli Prime Minister Menachem Begin together in the Mideast Peace Talks. He would eventually succeed, however, and an historic peace accord would be signed.

For Jimmy, things could indeed be worse.

Herman and Jimmy experience grueling reelection campaigns during the summer of 1980. Both would lose.

Sen. Herman Talmadge

The wife of political activist Julian Bond accuses him of using cocaine. One recalls that former senator Herman Talmadge's downfall began with accusations from an irate wife.

Over the years, with a declining population and tax base, Augusta depends more and more on double water rates from the unincorporated county to keep its financial ship afloat.

An Augusta Champion is honored.

The Iranian crisis in the Mideast fuels oil shortages. Quo vadis, America?

John Wayne, American, is dead.

At age 69, Ronald Reagan would become the oldest man ever elected president.

Ronald Reagan is sworn in as the 40th president of the United States.

Supply-side economic theory, which became better known as "Reaganomics", held that by cutting taxes, businesses and workers can keep and spend more of their earnings, thus enlarging the marketplace for all. Cuts in government spending should follow cuts in taxes and the chief target is domestic programs.

A major upset in Georgia. A Republican typewriter salesman from Brunswick, Mack Mattingly, defeats Sen. Herman Talmadge in a close Senate race.

Our county delegation heads for Atlanta and the Georgia General Assembly. From left: Rep. Jack Connell, Sen. Tom Allgood and Rep. Don Cheeks. Seated in sidecar: Rep. Mike Padgett, Sen. Jimmy Lester, Reps. Sam Nicholson and R.A. Dent and trailing behind, the lone Republican, Rep. David Swann.

The decade begins on an ominous note. Russia invaded Afghanistan in late 1979, and meeting determined resistance from guerrilla bands, pours manpower and material into the escalating conflict.

In 1988, the Soviets announce the withdrawal of their troops from Afghanistan, repeating the bitter lesson of America's Vietnam experience.

Basic Baseball 101. "Braves, this is a baseball. You hit it, you throw it, you catch it…

The Falcons are having trouble scoring points.

The proper labeling for local consumption would be; '' Savannah River Plant'' instead of ''waste storage site'', ''DOE'' instead of ''Feds'' and ''DuPont'' instead of ''nuclear industry''.

Led by Coach Erk Russell's ''Junkyard Dog'' defense and running back Herschel Walker, the ''Dawgs'' beat Notre Dame 17-10 in the Sugar Bowl and are proclaimed the 1980 National Champions.

The U.S. wins some gold and much-needed prestige in the 1980 winter Olympics.

Extreme unrest in Poland is led by the Solidarity trade union. Only crackdowns by the Communist puppet government, including the arrest of labor leader Lech Walesa, keep Soviet tanks from crossing the border.

Pope John Paul II visits his homeland, criticizing the military government and calling for more freedom for the Polish people.

Lawyer Jack Ruffin thwarts an effort by the Richmond County School Board to return to neighborhood schools.

Ruffin is later appointed Superior Court Judge.

On March 30, 1981, President Reagan is shot. Pope John Paul II is shot on May 13. Both men survived the attempted assassinations.

The third assassination attempt of the year is successful.

President Reagan sends U.S. Marines to Lebanon as part of a multinational peace-keeping force. A bomb-laden truck driven by a terrorist crashes into their headquarters, killing 241.

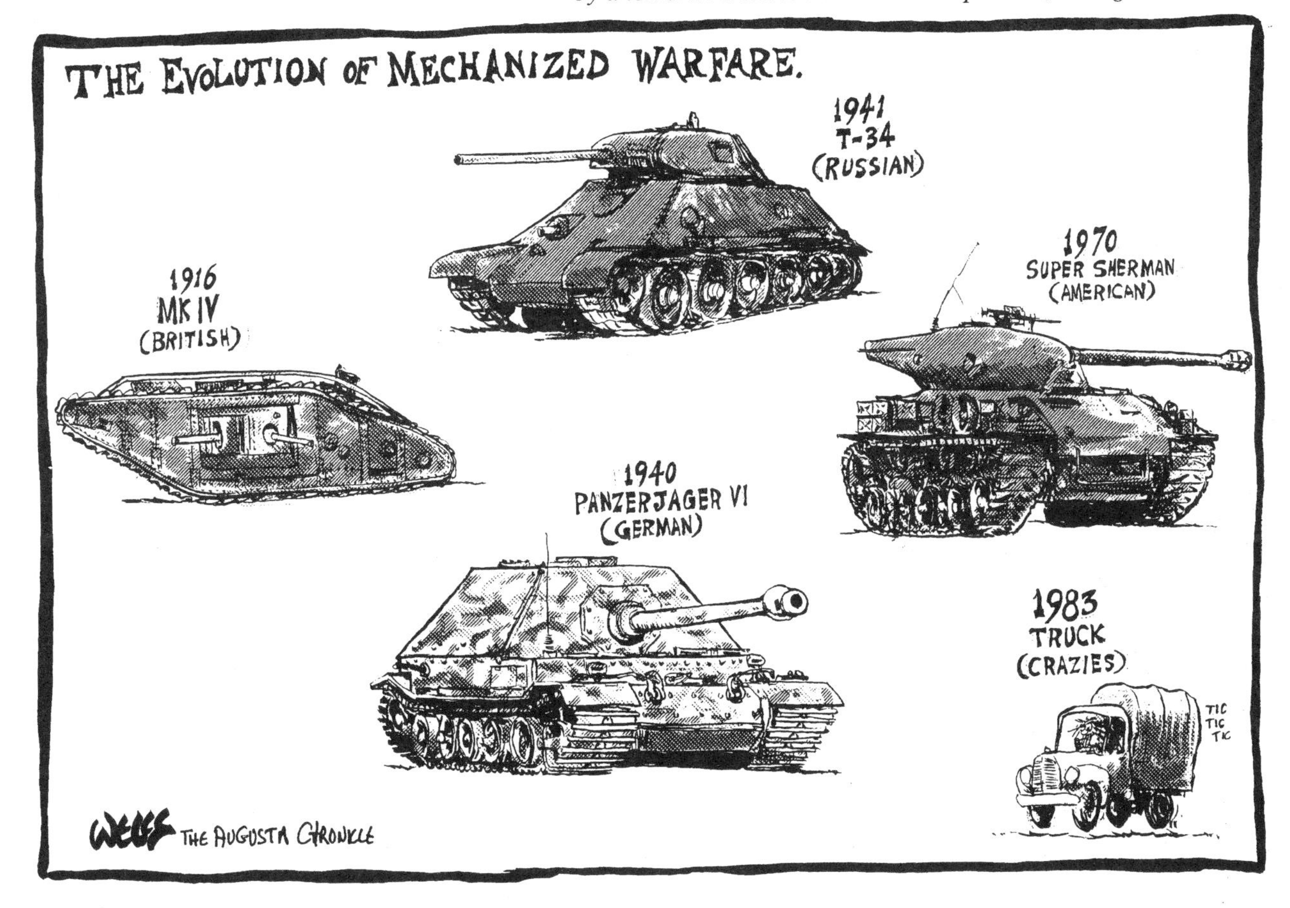

Mayor Newman is recognized for his wheeling and dealing of city land along the river for private development.

Bjorn Borg had just won his 5th consecutive Wimbledon Tennis title.

In 1972, Lewis A. (Pop) Newman was elected mayor of Augusta largely on the promise to rid the downtown of its many rail crossings. Herewith, a monument to his achievements.

Edward M. McIntyre is the new mayor. With three exceptions, he soon has city council voting his way.

²tacky\'tak-ē\ adj tack·i·er; -est 1 a: marked by lack of style or good taste: b: marked by cheap showiness
WELCOME TO
AUGUSTA
THE GARDEN CITY
EDWARD M. McINTYRE, MAYOR

At taxpayers' expense Mayor McIntyre replaces city limit signs with some more suitable to his personal taste.

Undercover FBI agents, posing as developers, nail Mayor Ed McIntyre and Councilman Joe Jones receiving kickbacks from riverfront developers.

An odd coalition on the Richmond County School Board combines to oust Superintendent William Oellerich.

Richmond County Sheriff J.B. Dykes is caught up in a ticket-fixing scheme and charges of obstruction of justice.

Some confusion as to whether George Washington's birthday is a legal holiday. Probate Judge Iree Pope is represented by Snow White.

Augusta has the dubious distinction of having its mayor, sheriff, district attorney and a city councilman either under indictment, in court or in jail. And those were just the ones that got caught.

R.A. Dent, the first black representative from Richmond County since Reconstruction, is dead.

The Clemson Tigers are the 1981 National Champions in football.

Herschel wins the big one.

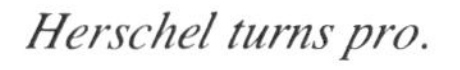

Herschel turns pro.

Ted Turner
media mogul and Braves owner.

The Atlanta Braves win the West but lose to the St. Louis Cardinals in the 1982 National League playoffs.

4 5 6 7 8 9 10 11
'The Scale'

Improprieties surface in the Human Relations Commission and Director Charles Walker takes his standard defense whenever he is criticized — racism. (Walker sued the newspaper for a Herald editorial and this cartoon. The suit was thrown out. Sad to say, it was the only law suit that I generated with thousands of cartoons drawn over the years.)

Heading for Atlanta are, from left: Don Cheeks, Charles Walker, George Brown, Mike Padgett (driving), Jack Connell, Jimmy Lester, Tom Allgood and Travis Barnes.

Two former sheriffs of Richmond County are in prison at the same time.

James Brown, the Godfather of Soul, fought the law and the law won. He is sentenced to serve hard time.

How much indeed! The defense budget continues to grow.

Led by Defense Secretary Caspar Weinberger, the national defense received high priority in the Reagan administration. It was OMB director David Stockman's job to apply some occasional restraint.

Reagan proposes a 1985 budget of $925.5 billion, with revenues of $745 billion.

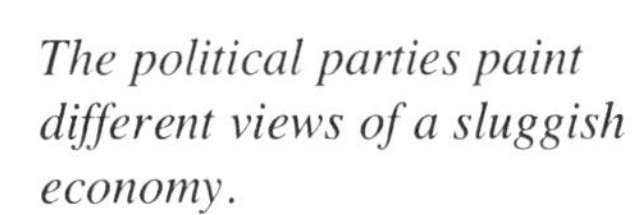

The political parties paint different views of a sluggish economy.

After losing in the 1980 presidential race in which both his competence and policies came under harsh attack, one could wonder if Carter could not but help taking some solace in the fact that Reagan was doing little better.

The deficit continues to grow on its merry way.

The Gramm-Rudman-Hollings Act is born. The goal of the law is to reduce the deficit in yearly increments until a balanced budget is achieved by fiscal 1993. It would not happen.

A star is born. Secretary of the Interior James Watt leads the administration's assault on the nation's resources. Environmental regulations are sharply reduced and billions of wilderness and offshore acres are opened to oil and gas drilling.

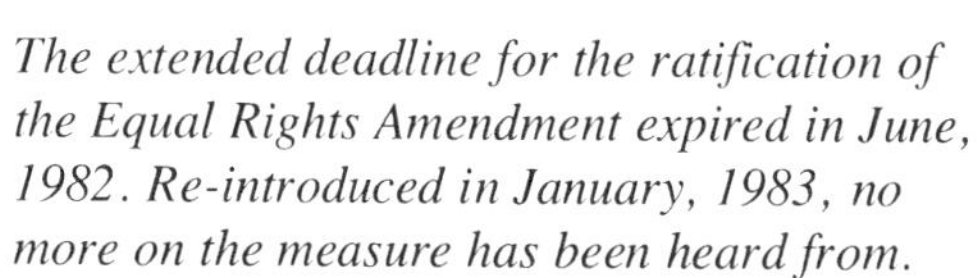

The extended deadline for the ratification of the Equal Rights Amendment expired in June, 1982. Re-introduced in January, 1983, no more on the measure has been heard from.

Though a survey showed that a majority of TV newscasters leaned toward the Democratic Party, the networks deny that television reporting is slanted.

Sandra Day O'Connor is the first woman to serve on the Supreme Court.

Sally Ride becomes the first American woman in space aboard the space shuttle Challenger.

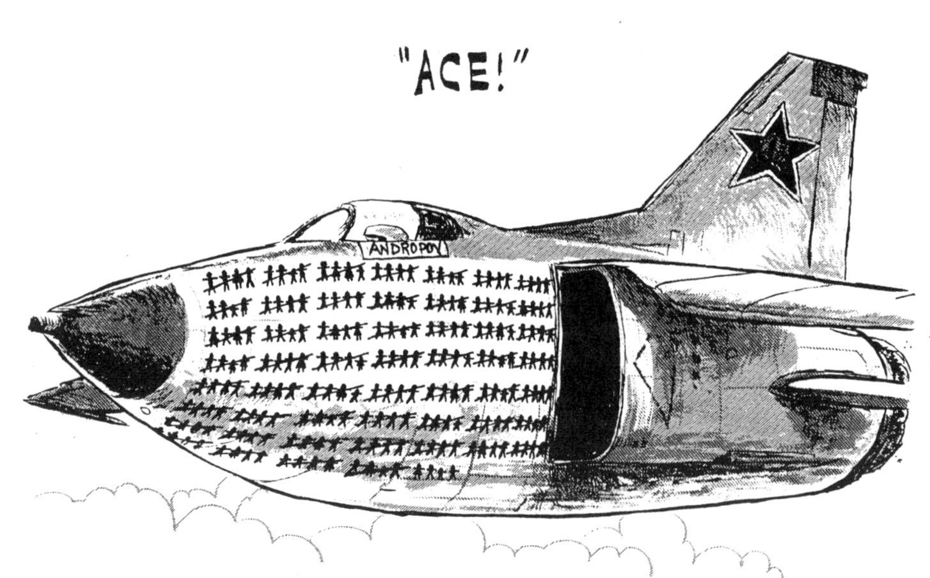

Korean Airlines Flight 007 is shot down by a Soviet fighter after accidentally straying into Russian airspace. All 269 passengers, including Georgia congressman Larry McDonald, are killed.

Argentina invades the Falkland Islands. Great Britain responds and prevails after ten weeks and the deaths of more than 1000 troops.

In late 1983, Jesse Jackson went to Syria and secured the release of an American airman shot down in Lebanon. Some months later, Atlanta Braves pitcher Paschal Perez is arrested in the Dominican Republic, allegedly for the possession of a mind-altering substance, threatening his status for the baseball season.

Gubernatorial candidate Bo Ginn charges Joe Frank Harris with impropriety in sales to government road-building programs from his cement plant. The charge backfired.

Joe Frank Harris is inaugurated as governor of Georgia.

Lt. Gov. Zell Miller, as presiding officer of the Senate, and Gov. Joe Frank Harris contemplate educational funding.

Two school issues come together.

Two old Democratic warhorses, Harrell Tiller and Mike Padgett, continue to exert their influence on the county commission.

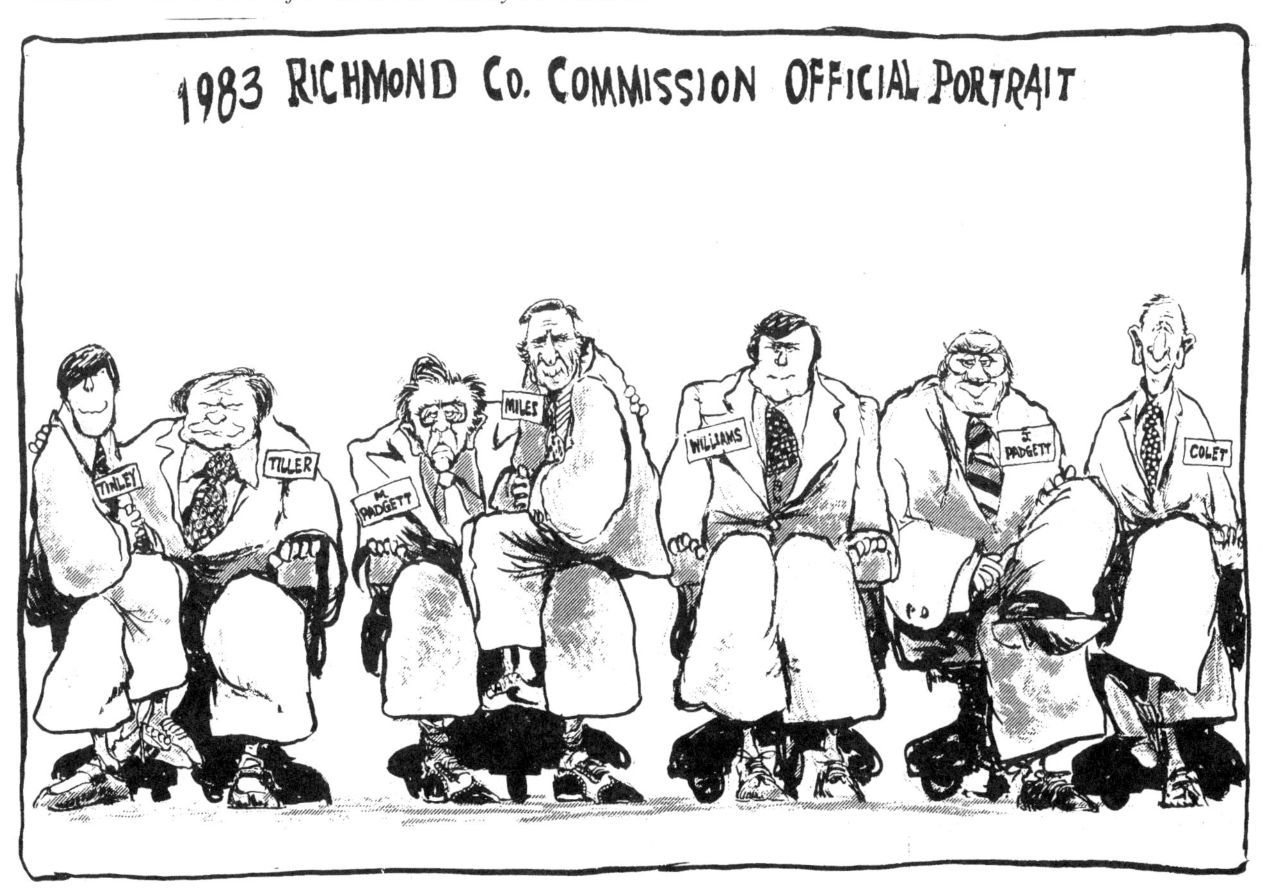

Craig Stadler

1982 Masters champion

Heavy rains hampered play in the 1983 Masters.

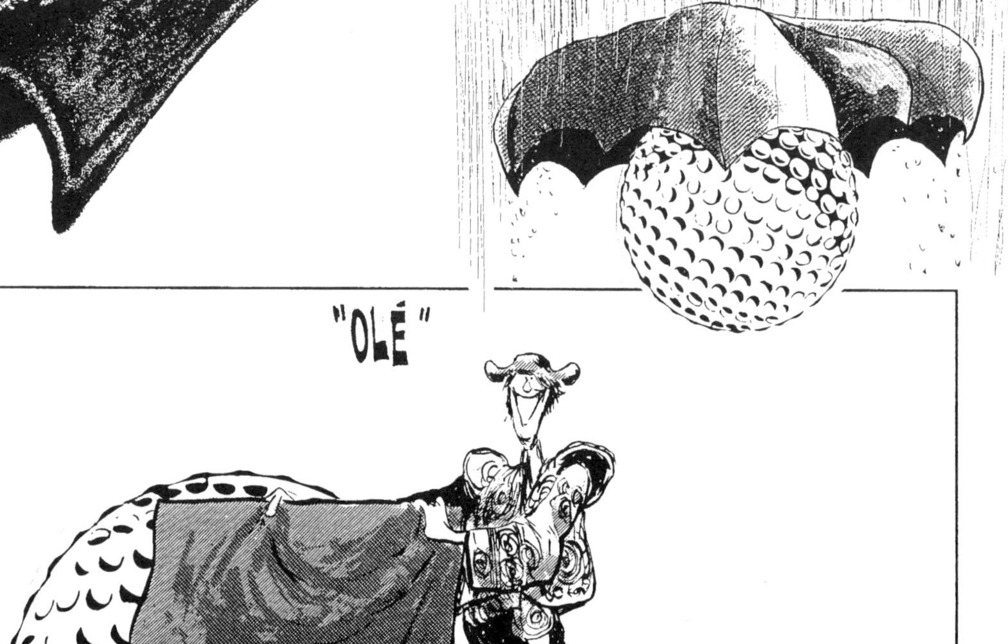

Masters champion in 1980 and 1983, Severiano Ballesteros prepares to defend his championships.

HOW 'BOUT ME!

Georgia beats Texas 10-9 in the Cotton Bowl.

The Georgia Tech Yellowjackets finish 9-2-1 in 1985 including a 17-14 win over Michigan State in the All-American Bowl.

Stung by critical editorials and cartoons in The Augusta Chronicle and Augusta Herald, Columbia County Sheriff Tom Whitfield retaliates by arresting editorial page editor Phil Kent on a trumped-up DUI charge. A few weeks later, Kent is viciously attacked by Whitfield's son and deputy, Bruce. Whitfield is voted out of office the next year.

Liberal nominee Walter Mondale finds less than enthusiastic support from Georgia's Democrats.

A sordid affair unfolds in the Reagan administration when it is learned that $30 million in profits from the sale of military equipment to Iran is channeled by the National Security Council to the Contras fighting to overthrow the Sandinista government in Nicaragua.

After a lengthy study of the Iran-Contra arms deal, the Tower Commission concludes that President Reagan's method of management was confused and out of touch with vital government programs.

All things considered, 1985 was not a banner year.

Most area cities comparable or smaller in size to Augusta appear to be able to support professional baseball.

Professional baseball in Augusta finds few fans in local political and business leaders.

Reprinted over the years on the annual occasion of the mathematical elimination of the Atlanta Braves in the National League pennant race.

Through the perseverance of Col. William ''Bill'' Heaton, Augusta finally gets a professional baseball team, the Pirates, later to be renamed the GreenJackets.

Billy Martin
Baseball player and manager

NEVER!
YES
OF COURSE.
OH ELL YES.
No...
maybe?
ABS LUTELY NOT
TOM
JIMMY
GEORGE
BILL
DON
JACK
TRAVIS
MIKE
CHARLES
GEN'L ASSEMBLY
WELLS
..AND HE IS THEM!
—WITH THANKS & APOLOGIES
TO POGO POSSUM & WALT KELLY

Seated front: Sen. Jimmy Lester, Reps. Bill Jackson, Jack Connell, Travis Barnes, Mike Padgett, and Charles Walker, Rear: Sen. Tom Allgood and Reps. George Brown, Don Cheeks and pole man, Pogo.

Mondale appoints Bert Lance as his campaign manager. It is a short-lived appointment.

Mondale selects Rep. Geraldine Ferraro of New York — the first woman in history to run as a vice-presidential running mate.

Grovetown enters a period of several years of non-stop recalls and elections. Ronald Reagan sweeps into a second term, losing only Minnesota and the District of Columbia.

Reagan cabinet officers

David Stockman
OMB Director

George Shultz
Secretary of State

Caspar Weinberger
Secretary of Defense

Jeane Kirkpatrick
Ambassador to the U.N.

West German Bernhard Langer wins the 1985 Masters. He would win again in 1993.

Lee Trevino continues his annual petty feud with the Augusta National.

Commissioners Henry Brigham, Henry Howard, Tom Tinley and Jesse Carroll with one of their more disturbing votes. Not pictured or involved are Commissioners Lee Neel and Herb Beckham.

Our four mouseketeers, with the aid of former top mouseketeer, Harrell Tiller, put out the welcome mat for the Masters.

Elected or appointed law chief? The people of Richmond County vote to vote for their sheriff.

WRDW news anchor Charley Britt reports a rumor that a black man has been beaten to death in the Burke County jail. It was only a rumor – an autopsy showed the man died from heat exhaustion – but a riot ensued in Waynesboro.

Another egg is laid, figuratively speaking, when the Coca Cola Company decides to change its 99-year-old Coke formula. The public doesn't buy it.

The petty politics of Grovetown continue to abuse and misuse Georgia's recall law.

Republicans Sen. Frank Albert and Reps. Jim Hill and Dick Ransom join the previously all-Democratic delegation.

The University Hospital Authority seeks a corporate restructure of the hospital which will diminish its accountability to the citizens of Richmond County — the ultimate owners. It succeeds but is subject to the provisions of Georgia's Open Records and Meetings Law.

Professor Jan Kemp complains about the coddling of athletes in the remedial studies program at the University of Georgia. She is fired.

Professor Kemp sues and wins reinstatement and a substantial financial settlement.

Coach Erk Russell accomplishes a near impossible feat. Starting from scratch, he builds the Georgia Southern Eagles into a national champion football team in four years. They would repeat as national champions in 1986.

The chairmanship passed from Tom Tinley to Henry Brigham (neither shown above.)

Mayor Charles DeVaney carries on an Augusta tradition.

House Speaker Thomas P. "Tip" O'Neill, D-Mass., retires after 34 years in Congress.

House Speaker
Tip O'Neill

At age 46, Jack Nicklaus wins his sixth Masters in 1986.

Libyan leader Moammar Gadhafi continues to sponsor and train terrorists. Ten days after a West Berlin nightclub is bombed killing two U.S. servicemen, Reagan orders an attack on Libyan targets where terrorists are being trained.

The worst nuclear power accident in history occurs when a reactor, out of control with a sudden burst of power, explodes at the town of Chernobyl in the Ukraine.

The months following her losing campaign were full of problems for former vice-presidential candidate Geraldine Ferraro. First her husband and then her son were intertwined with legal problems.

Tragedy! The space shuttle Challenger explodes just 73 seconds after launch. Dead are flight commander Francis Scobee, pilot Michael J. Smith, mission specialists Ellison Onizuka, Judith Resnik, and Ronald McNair, Hughes Aircraft engineer Gregory Jarvis, and schoolteacher Christa McAuliffe. A special commission's report calls for widespread reforms in NASA's operations.

A Piedmont 737 sets down at little Daniel Field.

Wyche Fowler defeats U.S. Senator Mack Mattingly in the 1986 senate race with some low road campaigning.

The FAA appears to be asleep at the switch as problems mount in the airline industry.

The gun-controllers continue to blame only the gun.

The Red Sox snatch defeat from the jaws of victory in the World Series against the Mets. A stunned Republican Party loses the Senate in the 1986 elections.

The mistreatment and abuse of animals in the city-run Atlanta Zoo becomes a national story and disgrace.

Andrew Young

What with the sordid conditions at the Atlanta Zoo and Amtrak's horrendous safety record…

In 1986, the Statue of Liberty celebrates her 100th birthday with a complete renovation and restoration.

The 200th anniversary of the U.S. Constitution is celebrated in 1987.

Surgeon General C. Everett Koop blankets the country with information and warnings about AIDS. The U.S. Public Health Service estimates that by 1992 some 380,000 people will have contracted the disease.

The controversy over how to halt the spread of AIDS (Acquired Immune Deficiency Syndrome) continues.

Frontrunner Gary Hart is forced to withdraw from the Democratic presidential nomination race because of his involvement with model Donna Rice.

At times, it appears that Nancy Reagan is the real power behind the president.

The Rhinestone Cowboy. — Some disillusionment among the Reaganites.

Reagan asked for and received a tax reform bill from Congress. Numerous deductions were wiped out, tax rates lowered and much of the tax burden was shifted from individuals to corporations. Most Americans seemed resigned to the fact that, in the end, they would be paying more taxes.

A fresh wind seems to be blowing from the Soviet Union in the person of General Secretary Mikhail Gorbachev, resulting in significant progress in slowing the arms race. President Reagan and Gorbachev meet in Geneva. Though Reagan refused to budge from his plans to proceed with his Strategic Defense Initiative, popularly known as "Star Wars," the Soviet leader agrees to scrap four weapons to America's one in Europe, resulting in 4,500 warheads to be destroyed.

Some disturbing revelations begin to surface st SRP.

DuPont announces it is ending its 35-year stewardship of the Savannah River Plant, leaving a dubious record of safety and environmental management.

Problems in Republican Sheriff Otis Hensley's department appear to lie in the minds of a Democratic county commission and district attorney in Columbia County. It would cost them in the next election. (That the good die young was certainly true in Hensley's case. He died in office. He was a good man and a good sheriff.)

Partisan politics also appear to enter the budget picture.

Some various and sundry problems of the community.

A University of Georgia management study indicates that the administration of the Augusta Police Department is in dire need of a professional administrator.

One of the most needed roadways in the state, the Murray Road Project, for years seems to be beyond the capabilities of Richmond County's powerful state politicians.

Augusta native Larry Mize wins the Masters with a dramatic chip-in on the 3rd playoff hole against Greg Norman.

''Black Monday,'' October 19 — the stock markets's worst crash since 1929. The Dow Jones Industrial Average dropped 508 points, 22.6 percent of its volume!

The drug lords are winning.

The challengers for the Democratic presidential nomination were dubbed the seven dwarfs. After Hart's pullout, polls show Jesse Jackson to be the frontrunner.

Sam Nunn decides not to run for president.

Jackson runs strong in the primaries and heads for the Democratic convention in Atlanta with hopes of gaining a spot on the ticket.

THE TORONTO SUMMIT ENDS ON A HIGH NOTE WITH A GENEROUS TOAST FROM ALL.
RED INK

Reagan's toast reflects a federal deficit that has reached almost $3 trillion.

HOSTAGE!
BUSH
IRAN
CONTRA

What did George know and when did he know it clouds the Bush presidential campaign.

I AM SOME BODY!
WE ARE SOME BODY!!
JESSE
BUSH

Leading big in the polls, George Bush deftly avoids the issues and runs as an extension of Ronald Reagan.

Conflicts of interest in business dealing by former Reagan aides continue to embarrass the president.

Georgia Republican congressman Newt Gingrich goes on an ethics witchhunt. House Speaker Wright is his chief victim.

Bobby Dodd was head football coach at Georgia Tech from 1945 to 1966. His teams compiled a 165-64-8 record including a 12-0 season and a national title in 1952. An All-American quarterback at Tennessee, Dodd joined Amos Alonzo Stagg as the only inductee to be enshrined into the National Football Foundation College Football Hall of Fame as both player and coach. Bobby Dodd died in 1988 at age 79.

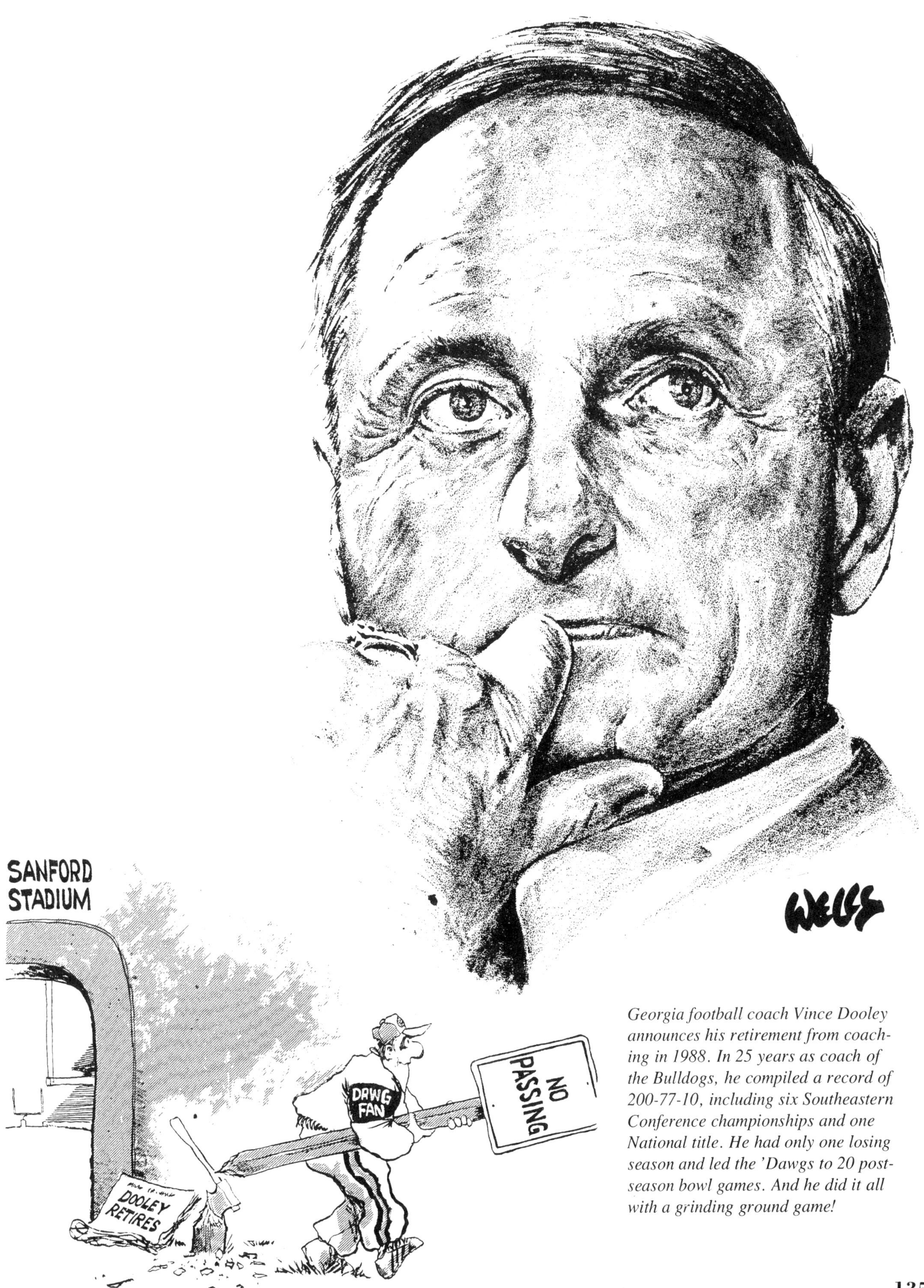

Georgia football coach Vince Dooley announces his retirement from coaching in 1988. In 25 years as coach of the Bulldogs, he compiled a record of 200-77-10, including six Southeastern Conference championships and one National title. He had only one losing season and led the 'Dawgs to 20 post-season bowl games. And he did it all with a grinding ground game!

For several days, former Georgia football coach Vince Dooley appears to be a bonafide and energetic candidate for governor — then suddenly, announces he will not run.

Augusta's Riverwalk is part of a long-reaching and splendid development of the city's riverfront. Across the river, North Augusta elects to install an above-ground sewer line.

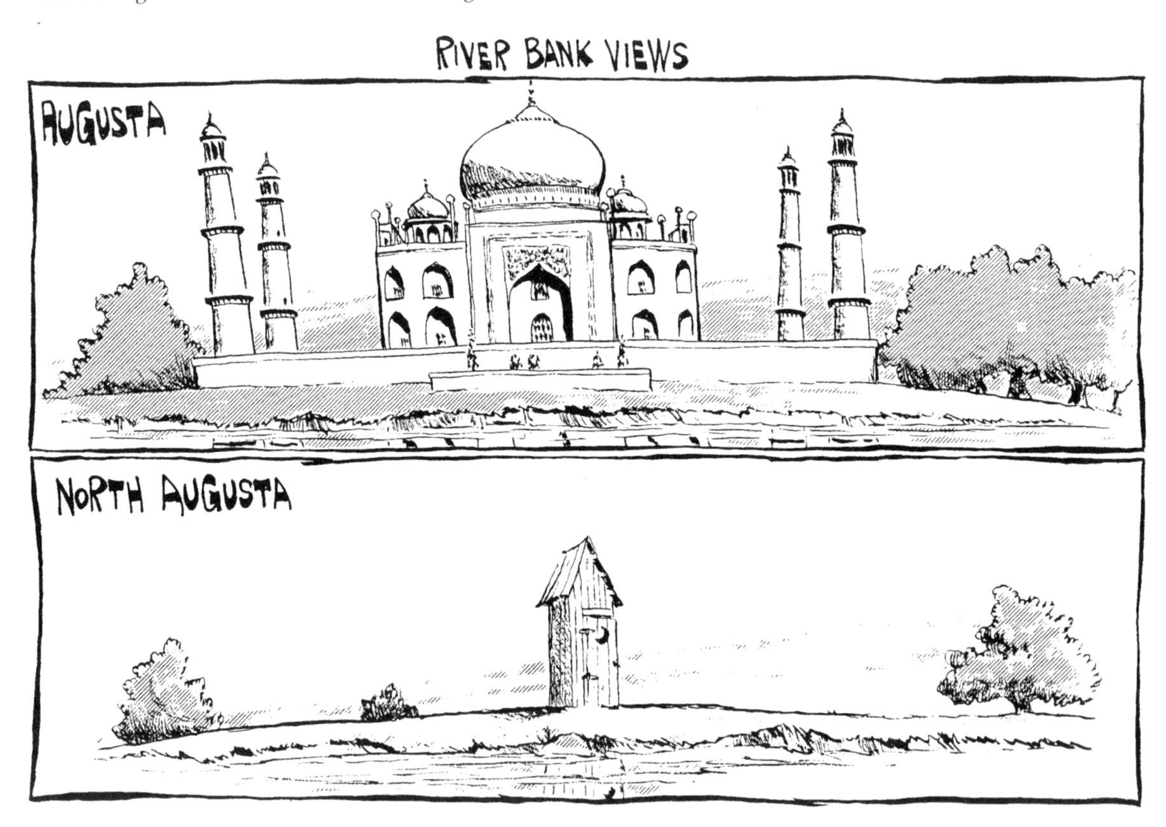

Rep. Jack Connell assumes his historical stance in opposing a consolidation bill (see page 33). He is joined by Mike Padgett and Dick Ransom.

Bruised but none the less for wear, the taters come on board and the people of Augusta and Richmond County get a consolidation bill to vote on.

The city continues its attempts to annex select areas of the county.

Michael Dukakis wins the nomination and selects Sen. Lloyd Bentsen of Texas as his running mate. In return for his support, Jackson receives concessions and an influential position in the campaign and the party, including access to party finances and the use of a jetliner. As one wag put it at the time, that is what any terrorist would receive – an airplane and money.

Rev. Jesse Jackson

Jackson proves to be not much of an asset to the Dukakis campaign.

During the campaign, Bush metaphorically refers to 1,000 points of light as an example of private enterprise, institutions and individuals helping those less fortunate. The electoral vote count in the election — Bush 426, Dukakis 112.

The Exxon oil tanker, Exxon Valdez, runs aground off the Alaskan coast, spilling millions of gallons of crude oil. Exxon's diligence in cleaning up the mess leaves a lot to be desired.

The Supreme Court legalizes the burning of the American flag.

It's Christmas time and escalating baseball contracts are under the tree.

BACK TO THE FUTURE

Two figures from the past emerge as possible political candidates. McIntyre loses to Sen. Tom Allgood. Lester opts not to run.

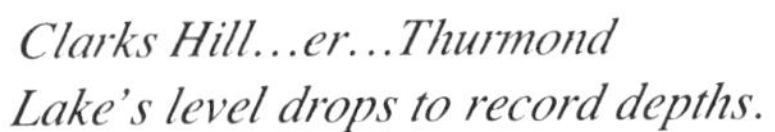

Clarks Hill…er…Thurmond Lake's level drops to record depths.

Joe Frank Harris imposes his fundamentalist religious convictions on the state by blocking legislation legalizing pari-mutuel wagering and a state lottery.

Concerns over safety shut down all three of SRP's aging reactors.

The fox (Dept. of Energy) is sent to guard the henhouse.

The fox was not a very good guard.

The war between Iran and Iraq officially ends.

Defrocked evangelist Jim Bakker and wife, Tammy the painted lady, almost regain control of the PTL organization.

Ayatollah Khomeini is dead.

George Bush is inaugurated as our 41st president.

Bush's relative inactivity in his first few months as president is well accepted. Polls give him a 70 percent approval rating.

1903 · PANAMA · 1989
BULLY!
CANAL CONST. BEGINS
T.R.
WELLS '89 THE AUGUSTA CHRONICLE

BULLY.
NORIEGA
FREE ELECTIONS

Indicted by a Florida grand jury for drug trafficking, strongman Gen. Manuel Noriega continues to thwart U.S. efforts to oust him.

In May, strongman Gen. Manuel Noriega throws out the returns of Panama's free elections. A few weeks later, the Justice Department does the same for Richmond County's consolidation vote.

FREE ELECTIONS AXED!..! HIGH FIVES ARE IN ORDER.
NORIEGA
JUSTICE DEPT.
CONSOLIDATION VOTE

BUG TALK
IT IS THE MOST STRANGEST THING. ONE MOMENT, MY NEW FRIEND, MANUEL NORIEGA AND I ARE SITTING ON OUR ROCKS IN THE SUN AND THE NEXT... POOF!! HE IS GONE!!
ORTEGA

Noriega declares a state of war exists between the U.S. and Panama. Following the killing of an American serviceman, the U.S. invades Panama and Noriega is turned over to U.S. authorities for trial on drug charges. He is found guilty and sentenced to prison. Ortega would follow a few years later, when, bowing to international pressure, he allows free elections and the Sandinistas are voted out of power.

The fortunes of the Communist bloc appear on the wane.

PLO leader Yasser Arafat's perennial solution to his problems with Israel.

Some progress in Central America — very little in the Mideast.

In late 1989, the Berlin Wall falls and socialist Eastern Europe looks west.

With the fall of the Soviet Union, a new problem emerges – nuclear proliferation.

BLOC PARTY

The countries of the Eastern Bloc smell the fruits of freedom.

Economic deterioration threatens to undermine Gorbachev's political reform movement, perestroika, during 1990, drastically reducing economic aid to Cuba after decades of propping up the Castro government.

Repressive measures taken by Russia and China make them dubious allies.

While the powers discuss the reunification of Germany…Germany reunifies.

Reforms set in motion by President F.W. de Klerk, including the freeing of imprisoned anti-apartheid leader Nelson Mandela, signal the end of government sanctioned segregation in South Africa.

Perhaps more correctly, it is the Communists who are crumbling in Russia.

THE RUSSIANS ARE CRUMBLING!!
THE RUSSIANS ARE CRUMBLING!!

THOSE WERE THE DAYS (SNIFF) OL' FRIEND...
WE THOUGHT..(SOB)..THEY'D NEVER END.....
APARTHEID
COMMUNISM

Crumbling is indeed the word for apartheid, communism as well as the Soviet Union.

Gambling, philandering, paternity suits, and drugs undermine the respect of big league ball players. The principals named here are stars Pete Rose, Wade Boggs, Steve Garvey and Dwight Gooden.

The British continue to dominate the Masters.

The financial "wizardry" of our county commission is exposed ...

...and the defense rests.

Several years of dedicated work remedies a failing grade.

Too many prisoners and the district attorney, county commission and the sheriff find themselves in hot water.

South Carolina's state government falls from grace.

Richmond County School Superintendent John Strelec is under fire from the school board.

From across the river comes some competition for Grovetown's political antics.

Long-long-long-awaited River Watch Parkway, extending downtown Reynolds Street along the Savannah River into Columbia County, is opened.

Horse Creek Valley volunteer firefighters fail to stop a fire on the Aiken-Augusta Highway because of no county waterlines.

A firehouse burns down…

…and the culprit is within.

The Keystone Kops are slandered. The antics of the Augusta Police Department would make them look good.

And the knife…er..buck stops in the chief s back.

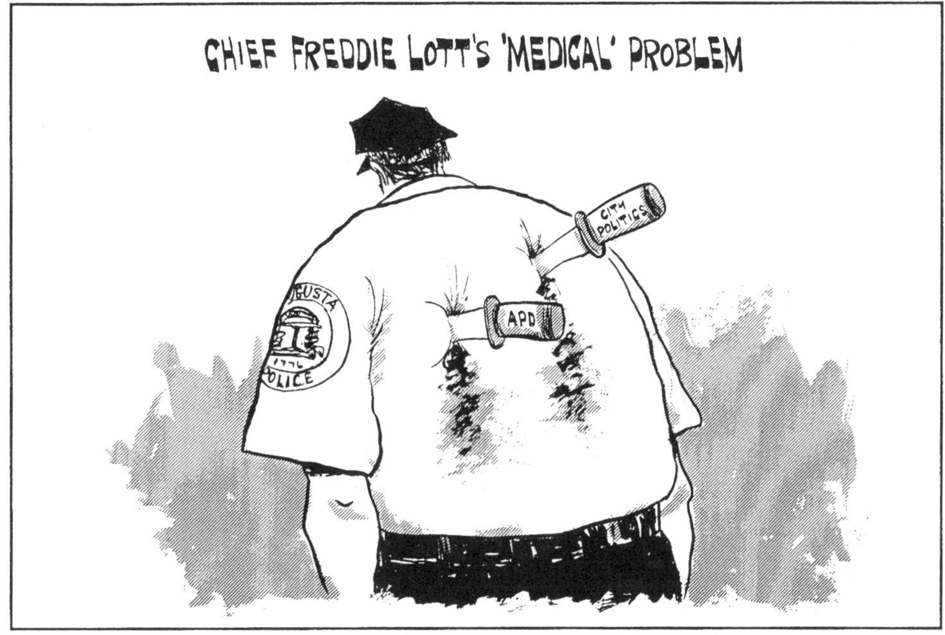

A new chief, Austin McLane, takes over and improvement is forthcoming.

Mayor Charles DeVaney is a vocal proponent of annexation. It appears to be a different matter with consolidation.

Another city-county fight threatens the construction of a new baseball stadium.

Local barbecue baron arrives on the political scene.

Clarence Thomas was nominated by President Bush to fill the vacancy created by the retirement of Supreme Court Justice Thurgood Marshall. Being a staunch conservative, Thomas was faced with a bitter confirmation fight within the Democratic-controlled Senate Judiciary Committee.

The hearings were further complicated when a young law professor, Anita Hill, testified that Thomas had sexually harrassed her ten years earlier when she worked for him.

Sen. Alan Cranston of California was among five U.S. senators alleged to have pressured regulators to show favoritism to convicted S&L magnate Charles Keating, Jr.

Twelve years of conservative Republican presidents produces, what else, a conservative Supreme Court.

Col. Oliver North is convicted on three felony counts of aiding the Reagan administration to deceive Congress in the arms-for-hostages initiative in Iran. The convictions are thrown out on a technicality.

Census reports show that poverty and income inequality rose to their highest level in 25 years. During the current recession 40 states reduced benefits for aid to families with dependent children, 30 states cut short-term assistance to the poor and 20 states reduced aid to the homeless — all complicated by a tight federal budget and huge deficits.

The House bank had quietly handled 8,331 bad checks written by congressmen that amounted to interest-free loans. This revelation followed by a few months U. S. congressmen quietly and quickly voting themselves a $23,000 pay raise.

Sidestepping the Gramm-Rudman-Hollings Act, Congress passed a controversial tax increase. Bush, who had run on a ''Read my lips, no new taxes'' platform in 1988, capitulated and signed on.

Economic recovery gives mixed signs.

The Democrats gain ground in the 1990 congressional elections.

Trade deficits with U-Know-Who continue to grow.

Receiving mixed signals from the State Department, Iraq invaded neighboring Kuwait on August 2, 1990. By year's end, President Saddam Hussein's occupying force totaled more than 500,000 armed troops poised on the border of oil-rich Saudi Arabia. The United Nations gave Saddam a January 15 deadline to pull out of Kuwait. Saddam ignored both a UN-sanctioned embargo and the January 15 deadline. U.S. and Allied troops launched bombing and missile strikes against Iraq. It was a rout. Opponents of the war believed it to be more a defense of Mideast oil rather than a war of liberation.

Saddam announces it to be a 'holy war' and the 'mother of all battles'.

YEA TEAM! WE'RE BEHIND YOU ALL THE WAY!!
RAH RAH TEAM! WE'RE WITH YOU NOW!
FOWLER
NUNN

For various reasons, Georgia's two senators opposed the war, but became supporters once hostilities began.

MR. PRESIDENT, MILITARY ACTION AGAINST IRAQ IS JUSTIFIED...

...BUT IT WOULD BE UNWISE.

HEADS I WIN, TAILS YOU LOSE.
NUNN for PRESIDENT IN '92

Nunn's rather nebulous reasoning, by his own admission, would rule out a run for the presidency in 1992.

Laser-guided bombs give new meaning to pin-point accuracy.

The Iraqi Air Force is a no-show. Most flew their aircraft into Iran and abandoned them.

Gen. Norman Schwarzkopf executes a textbook campaign, sweeping around Iraqi positions and cutting off reinforcements and supplies.

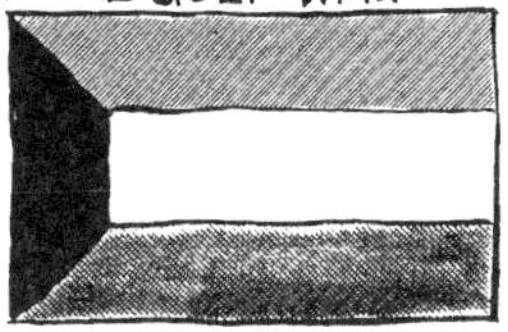
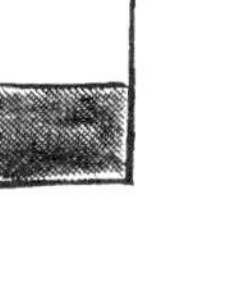

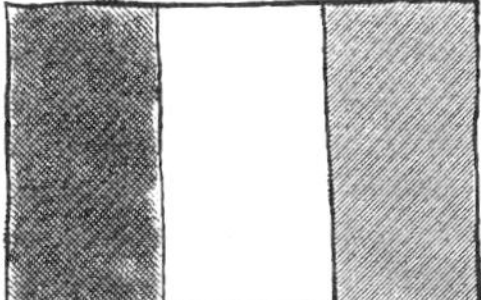

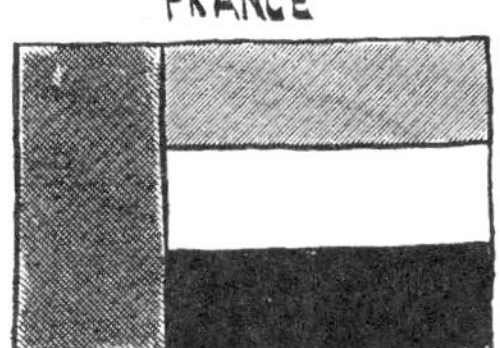

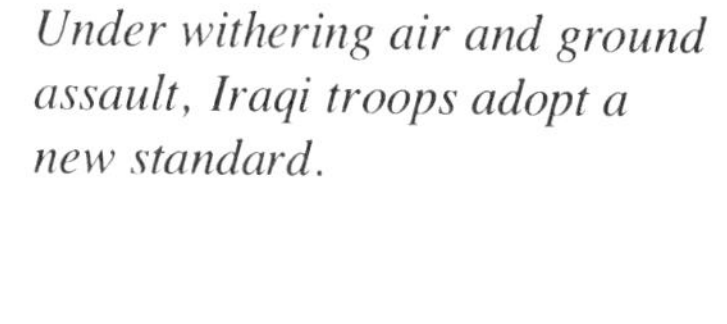

Under withering air and ground assault, Iraqi troops adopt a new standard.

The financial burden of the war falls chiefly on the United States. Japan's support leaves much to be desired.

Allied casualties were remarkably light, and America welcomes the troops home with parades and jubilation — in contrast to a war of another generation.

Saddam unleashes his troops to slaughter the tribal Kurds in the mountains of northern Iraq.

In 1991, William Kennedy Smith was charged with rape in Palm Beach following a bar-hopping soiree with Uncle Ted. To protect her identity, the face of the accuser was electronically distorted in TV court room coverage. Young Smith was acquitted, but in a surprising speech some weeks later at Harvard, the senator took responsibility for "faults in the conduct of my private life."

Financial institutions continue to prosper as the country struggles with economic recovery.

A free trade agreement with Mexico, NAFTA, draws opposition.

The Masters attracts the usual contingent of the world's top golfers.

After years of frustration on the state sports front, Atlanta is awarded the site of the 1996 Summer Olympics.

Legislation limiting quotas in hiring, contracts and education is contested in the senate. A modified version is passed.

For several years, New York Gov. Mario Cuomo commanded top attention as Democratic presidential possibility. He tarried, hesitated and would announce he would not run in 1992.

Base closings became a key component of defense cuts. Georgia has a 900-pound gorilla defending its bases.

After years of losing, the Braves win the 1991 National League pennant and the Falcons make the playoffs.

Deion Sanders flits between the two teams.

The NFL threatens to move the 1993 Super Bowl from Phoenix after Arizona voters fail to designate Martin Luther's birthday as a state holiday.

A powerful Georgia Tech football team finds itself in big company.

The Yellowjackets finish the season with 11-0-1 record including a 45-21 win over Nebraska in the Florida Citrus Bowl. They are proclaimed 1990 national champions.

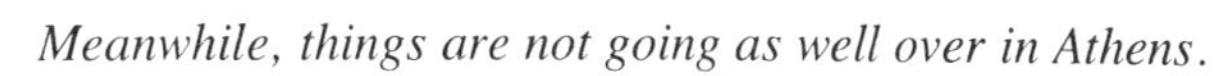
Meanwhile, things are not going as well over in Athens.

Arkansas governor Bill Clinton wins the 1992 Democratic nomination for president, but is dogged by allegations of infidelity. Clinton and his wife Hillary declare the issue to be irrelevant and she pledges her devotion and support.

The ACLU in its ever vigilant defense of individual rights, challenges a religious display on public property.

Riding high on the global economic scene, a Japanese official shares his rather succinct reasoning.

THE UNSUNG HEROES OF TODAY'S
BROAD STREET LONGHORN CATTLE DRIVE.

As a prelude to the annual Augusta Futurity, the inaugural longhorn cattle drive brings dedicated spadework from city employees.

Yet another reactor restart at Savannah River Plant…er…Site.

State Sen. Charles Walker becomes a major power broker on the Augusta political scene.

Its called self-serving quid pro quo or you scratch my back and I'll scratch yours.

Mayor DeVaney attempts to carry on the tradition of interfering with Augusta police chiefs.

The mayor becomes a globe-trotter.

REPS. GEORGE BROWN AND JACK CONNELL DISCUSS REDRAWING HOUSE DISTRICT LINES.
WHITE
BLACK
GEO.
JACK

Redrawing Georgia's district lines becomes a black-white issue.

YOU CAN RUN ALONG HOME NOW, JACK... THE SESSION'S OVER.

REP. CONNELL. COULD YOU COMMENT ON YOUR INVOLVE-MENT WITH THE $2,300,000 'TOM MURPHY' SLUSH FUND.
THAT WAS DUE TO CLERICAL ERRORS.
CLERICAL ERRORS?!? AREN'T YOU NOW REFERRING TO THE BOTCHED LOCAL SALARY BILL YOU CO-SPONSORED?
THAT WAS SUPPOSSED TO BE SECRET.
SECRET?!? DON'T YOU MEAN THE SLUSH FUND WAS SUPPOSSED TO BE SECRET?
YES! YES!
...AND THE SALARY BILL WAS CLERICAL ERRORS?..
YES!.. ...NO!?!
SAY GOODNIGHT, JACK.
GOODNIGHT JACK.

One could hardly be faulted with the assumption that, over the years, Rep. Jack Connell has been more attentive to House Speaker Tom Murphy's agenda than with that of his constituents of Augusta's Georgia House District 115.

Beginning with Sandy Lyle's win in 1988, the British won four consecutive Masters Championships. Nick Faldo won in 1989 and 1990 and Ian Woosnan was the champion in 1991.

County Administrator Robert Dixon is fired but he doesn't go peacefully, demanding (and getting) numerous severance benefits and perks.

From left:Commissioners Lee Neel, Don Grantham, Larry Sconyers and Hobson Chavous.

With some clandestine backing, Augusta's black leadership succeeds in getting consolidation overturned by the Justice Department.

LA. LAW

A jury hands down a verdict of "not guilty" in the case of four Los Angeles policemen caught on camera clubbing Rodney King while making an arrest.

Protesters rampaged through the city, looting and setting more than 5,000 fires. Fifty-eight people are killed.

LAPD suffers a loss of confidence.

The United Way also suffers because of lavish and extravagant spending in charity's national executive suites.

Questions arise as to our marksmanship in Operation Desert Storm.

In 1990 'Zig' Zell promises to serve only one term as governor. Two years later 'Zag' Zell announces for another campaign.

Political machinations aside, only a robust economy would ever deliver a solution.

TV character Murphy Brown gives birth to an out-of-wedlock baby. Illegitimacy being a major social problem, Vice President Dan Quayle criticizes the 'blessed event', thus inviting the invective of the 'Hollywood Left.'

Johnny Carson retires after thirty years.

It has since been determined that the economic recovery began in March 1991 but was not recognizable by the campaign summer of 1992.

George gets the nomination but fails to get the expected 'bounce' from the convention.

A no-confidence vote from the consumer.

A 14-year old boy in Florida goes to court and literally ''divorces'' his natural parents. Millions of Americans are similarly unhappy with government gridlock and politicians in general. Feeding on this disillusionment, Texas billionaire computer magnate, Ross Perot, gets enough signatures to be placed on the ballots of a majority of states. Abruptly withdrawing from the race at one point, the erratic Perot returns and pulls nineteen percent of the vote, the highest percentage for a third party candidate since Theodore Roosevelt.

A minor trade problem with les French.

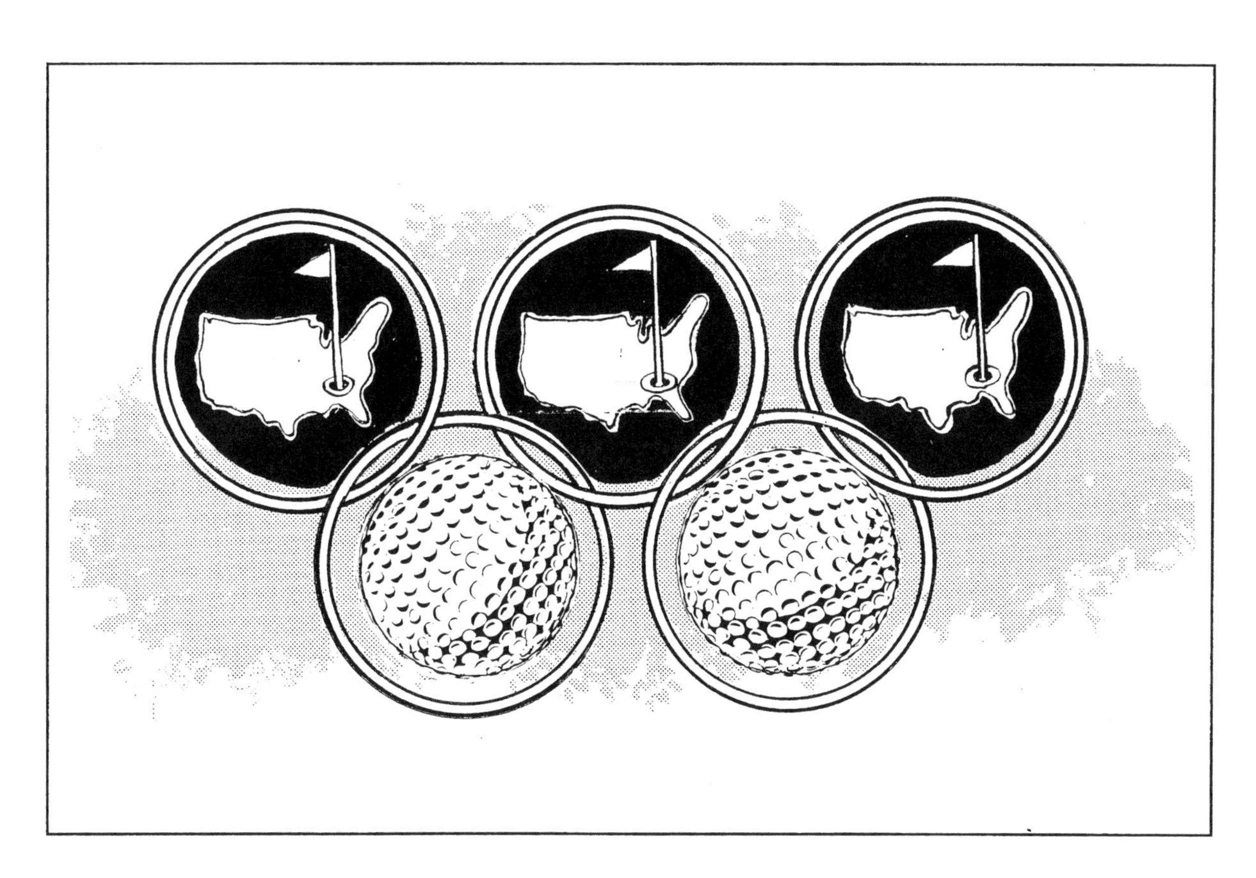

The Augusta National Golf Club offers the golf course as the site for the inaugural Olympic event for golf. The Atlanta City Council, led by its president, Bill Campbell, opposes the venue because of the supposedly 'racist and elitist' nature of the golf club. Because of the controversy, the Olympic committee cancels the event — a tragedy for golf, for the Olympics and for Georgia.

The official Olympic mascot, Izzy is not well received by the public.

1986
MY OPPONENT IS AFRAID TO DEBATE ME BECAUSE HE HAS TO HIDE HIS RECORD FROM GEORGIA VOTERS!!
MR. FOWLER

Lowlights of the Wyche Fowler-Paul Coverdell senate race of 1992. Coverdell wins in a squeaker.

After several attempts, St. Petersburg, Fla., fails to get a major league baseball franchise even though the city presumptively constructed a big league stadium. Their optimism would pay off a few years later.

Georgia running back
Garrison Hearst

American troops were sent to Somalia in late 1992 by President Bush, primarily to feed a starving population caused by warring warlords. During 1993, over thirty Americans and dozens of UN troops are killed.

Candidate Clinton pushes the usual Democratic agenda....

...while arch-conservative Pat Buchanan's campaign fizzles.

A stamp for Elvis. Would it be a 'young' Elvis or an 'old' Elvis?

As expected, Jesse Jackson enters the Democratic presidential sweepstakes…

…and comes up a little short.

The polls call it. The Bush campaign is DOA.

Though difficult to perceive, the recovery had begun in March, 1991. It was too late to save George Bush. Democrat Bill Clinton is the new president of the United States.

The respective pets have no problem with the transfer of power.

The new president leaves a trail of broken promises.

Pinched by the stagnant economy, some of the country's largest corporations suffer drastic downsizing.

Sensing a shift in the people's mood, the Democrats move a tad toward the center.

Gov. Zell Miller announces that he will lead a campaign to change the Georgia state flag, which contains the Confederate battle flag.

Though a vast majority of blacks were for the change, the majority of Georgians were vehemently opposed. Zell quits the flag-change crusade.

The new Washington residents decide that D.C.'s schools are not the place for their young daughter.

I WANT YOU TO SERVE IN THE
U.S. MILITARY AND KEEP YOUR SEX LIFE PRIVATE & SEPARATE AS IT SHOULD BE!!

President Clinton jumps into the controversy of gays serving in the military. Led by Sen. Nunn, powerful chairman of the Senate Armed Services Committee, the 'Don't ask, don't tell' policy becomes the order of the day.

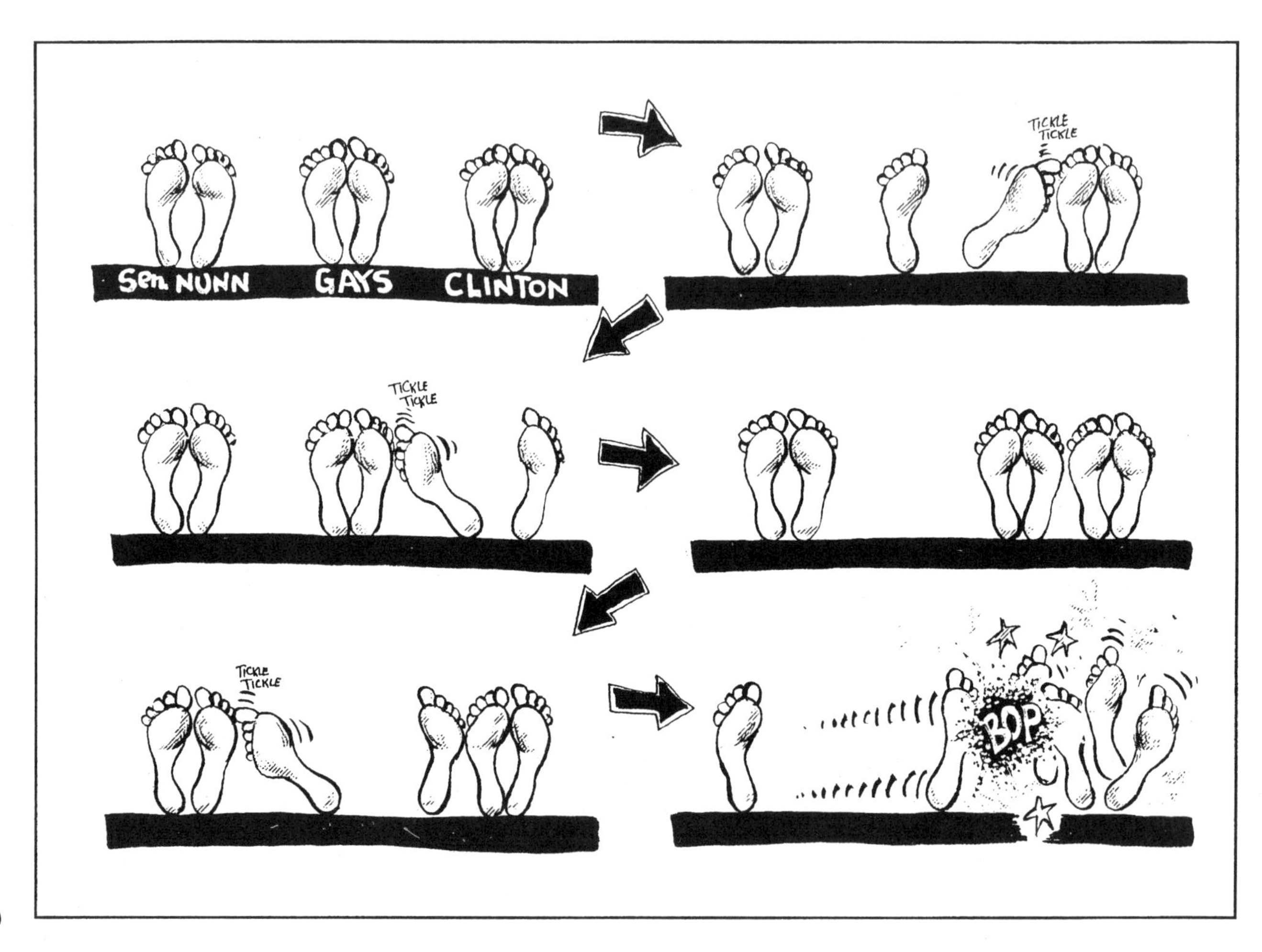

Hen's teeth are plentiful compared to Masters badges.

Arnold Palmer
Masters Champion 1958-60-62-64

State Senator Charles Walker and Mayor Charles DeVaney form a political partnership that appears, at times, to be serving them rather than the public.

The Augusta Herald folds after 102 years.

With little apparent foresight or feasibility studies of the local luxury condominium market, the Port Royal complex on the river in downtown Augusta is built for $40 million. Only seven of 56 units are sold. Those remaining are sold for $5.2 million, units are reduced by over 60 percent and sales have picked up.

Clinton's approval ratings plummet as the realities of the job set in. Poorly-conceived legislative initiatives, controversies and broken promises don't help matters.

A reminder throughout the Clinton campaign was, 'It's the economy, stupid.'

Will the bull market run forever? With brief interruptions, it sometimes appears so.

In Haiti, strongman Lt. Gen. Raoul Cedras ousts the elected president, Jean-Bertrand Aristide. With UN backing, President Clinton threatens military intervention. Cedras eventually backs down and Aristide is restored to office. Is Bosnia next?

The breakup of Yugoslavia brings about Europe's worst fighting since World War II in Bosnia.

U.S. military leaders, fearing another no-win Vietnam policy, resist involving American troops. The slogan is in reference to Clinton's draft dodging during the 1960s.

Over bitter labor opposition, Clinton and House Minority Whip Newt Gingrich, along with Senate Minority Leader Bob Dole, combine forces to pass the North American Free Trade Agreement. Wife Hillary would not be as successful with her health-care proposals.

Clinton emulates his Democratic predecessor.

Failure to pay domestic employees' Social Security taxes would side-track several Clinton nominations.

Local government receives a grant for almost $2 million to build sidewalks, primarily for the safety of children walking to school. Sen. Walker promptly hires a sidewalk construction superintendent (with no known experience in sidewalk construction), who, just as promptly hires workers from the senator's temporary employment agency, and promptly begins constructing sidewalks of dubious quality.

Not to be outdone, state Rep. Henry Howard brings his political influence into the capitalist marketplace of gospel singing.

County Attorney Robert C. Daniel once again renders a legal opinion that gets government officials off the hook. (Bobby Daniel was another able and competent public official who would die too young.)

Doing business with the sheriff.

Learning a business lesson, little New Ellenton faces default on an overly ambitious sewer project.

Doing business with the public's business.

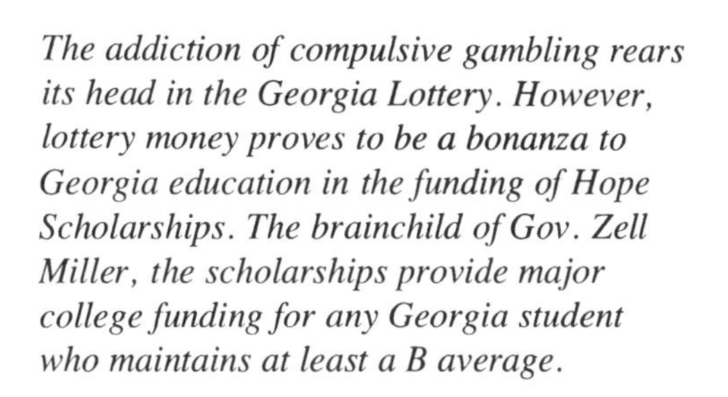

The addiction of compulsive gambling rears its head in the Georgia Lottery. However, lottery money proves to be a bonanza to Georgia education in the funding of Hope Scholarships. The brainchild of Gov. Zell Miller, the scholarships provide major college funding for any Georgia student who maintains at least a B average.

Blessed be the hypocrites.

South Carolina quenches its gambling fever with video poker.

Saddam Hussein defied the UN no-fly zone and attacked the Kurdish rebels. Clinton responded with cruise missiles and receives a show of support.

The U.S. Congress rightly does to China what the Atlanta City Council wrongly had done to Augusta.

In their patented late-season charge, the Braves overtake the San Francisco Giants and win the National League West.

The Braves lose the playoffs to the Philadelphia Phillies. The Phillies' good baseball is offset by unshaven, tobacco-stained chins and general sloppiness.

Deion leaves the Braves and signs on with Marge Schott's Cincinnati Reds.

A GATHERING OF CLOWNS

A rash of murders of foreign tourists stuns Florida and threatens the state's tourism industry.

Clinton pushes through one of the largest tax increases ever, but surprisingly to critics, it does not slow the recovering economy.

Immigration, both legal and other, becomes a flood that threatens to overflow the melting pot.

With the city heading for bankruptcy, the mayor attempts to bolster revenues, with Richmond County as his customer.

An excessive amount of police manhours are spent in a crackdown on prostitution in Olde Town.

McIntyre enters the 1993 mayoral race…

…but the courts say no way.

After ruling out a 10th District congressional run, Mayor DeVaney inspires Rep. Jack Connell to introduce a bill to increase his mayoral term from three to four years. (I believe this to be the only instance in which I put myself in a cartoon.)

GOP wins around the country portend the Republican sweep of Congress in 1994.

Kids continue to kill kids.

Illegitimate births continue to rise.

Clinton continues to move to the right of center.

It is revealed in 1994 that Ronald Reagan has Alzheimer's Disease. He would live out his life in virtual seclusion.

As usual, the city strives to not be outdone by the county.

Ice figure skater Tonya Harding conspires to have rival Nancy Kerrigan clubbed on the knee, thus enhancing Harding's chance to win a spot on the 1994 U.S. Olympic team. At about this time, the mayor comes skating by with, what else?, another annexation proposal.

Popular columnist, humorist and UGA 'Dawg', Lewis Grizzard, is dead.

Columbia County's justice..er..legal system in session.

'SEEING THE DELICIOUS DEER FOOD BESIDE THE FOREST PATH, BAMBI CRIED, "MOTHER. SHOULDN'T WE BE CAREFUL? THIS DELICIOUS DEER FOOD COULD HAVE BEEN PUT HERE BY HUNTERS!"
"OH, NO, SON. THAT IS ILLEGAL, AND BESIDES, WE'RE OUT OF SEASON."
HARDLY HAD THEY BEGUN MUNCHING THE DELICIOUS DEER FOOD, WHEN SUDDENLY, SHOTS RANG OUT!
BLAM! BAM! KA-POW! BANG!
DOWN WENT BAMBI! DOWN WENT HIS MOTHER!
LATER, CRUISING DOWN THE INTER-STATE WITH BAMBI AND HIS MOTHER SECURELY TIED ACROSS THE HOOD OF THEIR PICKUP, ONE HUNTER STATED, "I HOPE WE DON'T GET CAUGHT."
"NOT TO WORRY," THE OTHER HUNTER SAID. "WITH JUDGE PAT HARDAWAY ON THE BENCH, WE'VE NOTHING TO WORRY ABOUT."
THEY BOTH LAUGHED AND HUNTED ILLEGALLY FOREVER AFTER.'

Some fingers get caught in the county cash-advance till.

Yes.

Vacillation in Bosnia.

South African blacks voted for the first time on April 26, 1994, ending the policy of apartheid in that country. Nelson Mandela, for many years a prisoner of the government, was elected president. The Bosnian Serbs prefer the killing fields.

Following an historic Israeli-Palestinian peace agreement, a viable Palestinian self-government becomes a possibility.

Sen. Robert Packwood's amorous adventures come to light. He would be forced to resign from the Senate.

Welfare costs soar. Reform is considered.

Trade talks with the Japanese get nowhere.

The bull market's only enemy seems to be interest rate increases.

Oliver North 'fesses up.

Gangsta rap uses gutter-type and anti-police lyrics. The other fellow's lyrics are well known.

THE REPUTATION OF A MAN IS
LIKE HIS SHADOW: IT SOMETIMES
FOLLOWS AND SOMETIMES PRECEDES
HIM—IT IS SOMETIMES SHORT
AND SOMETIMES LONG.
—FRENCH PROVERB

RICHARD MILHOUS NIXON
1913-1994

Richard Nixon is dead at age 81.
His wife, Pat, died in 1993.

In a little over a year, using insider information, Hillary Rodham Clinton (as she prefers to be called) parlayed $1000 into a $100,000 profit in trading cattle futures.

Foreign policy is not the president's long suit.

Hillary Rodham's approval rating is not what it's cracked up to be.

Secretary of State
Warren Christopher

Name calling in the '90s.

Powerful congressman Dan Rostenkowski of Illinois is hit with a 17-count indictment, including taking unlawful privileges and converting postage stamps into cash. He is defeated for reelection and, pleading guilty to mail fraud, is sentenced to 17 months in prison.

Trashing the rules.

ORIENT EXPRESSIONS

The Fiftieth Anniversary of the Allied landing on the beaches of Normandy.

She ain't seen nothing yet. Wait til O.J.

In a crime that shocked the nation, football, TV and movie star O.J. Simpson is charged with brutally murdering his ex-wife, Nicole, and her friend, Ronald Goldman.

The bungling of evidence by the Los Angeles Police Department would seriously impede the investigation of the case.

It is brought out that Nicole Simpson was physically abused by her husband, spotlighting a longtime problem in the cavalier attitude of law enforcement to spousal abuse.

Federal Reserve Chairman Alan Greenspan's policy of manipulating interest rates to modify fluctuations in economic cycles appears to be remarkably successful.

And the bear has to bide his time.

A short-lived attempt to reign in juvenile crime by opening gyms for midnight basketball.

White House security is questioned when a pilot crashes his small plane into a tree a few yards from the Oval Office, and a gunman sprays the White house with semi-automatic rifle fire.

The delegation begins the arduous process of hammering out a new consolidation bill. Walker's feature would prevail, much to the dismay of future mayors.

Leadership comes from other than the delegation leader.

Sen. Walker does a 180 on consolidation. He pushed the black agenda and compromises on both sides lead to a bill for the citizens of Richmond County and Augusta to vote on.

Shenanigans down in Hephzibah town rival their bigger cousins.

A new consolidation bill passes and is promptly forwarded to the Justice Department. Hephzibah opts not to join.

The downtown rail crossing saga continues with the mayor issuing a traffic ticket to a railroad engineer for obstructing traffic on Sixth Street.

Two county commissioners get stuck in a road-paving spending quagmire. They would both lose their seats.

Like Clinton, Zell usurps most of the Republican agenda and wins. It was another matter for Tenth District congressman Don Johnson. He had cast the deciding vote in the president's tax increase bill after vowing not to vote for it. He faces Augusta dentist Charlie Norwood in the General Election. The appointment was painful. Johnson loses bigtime.

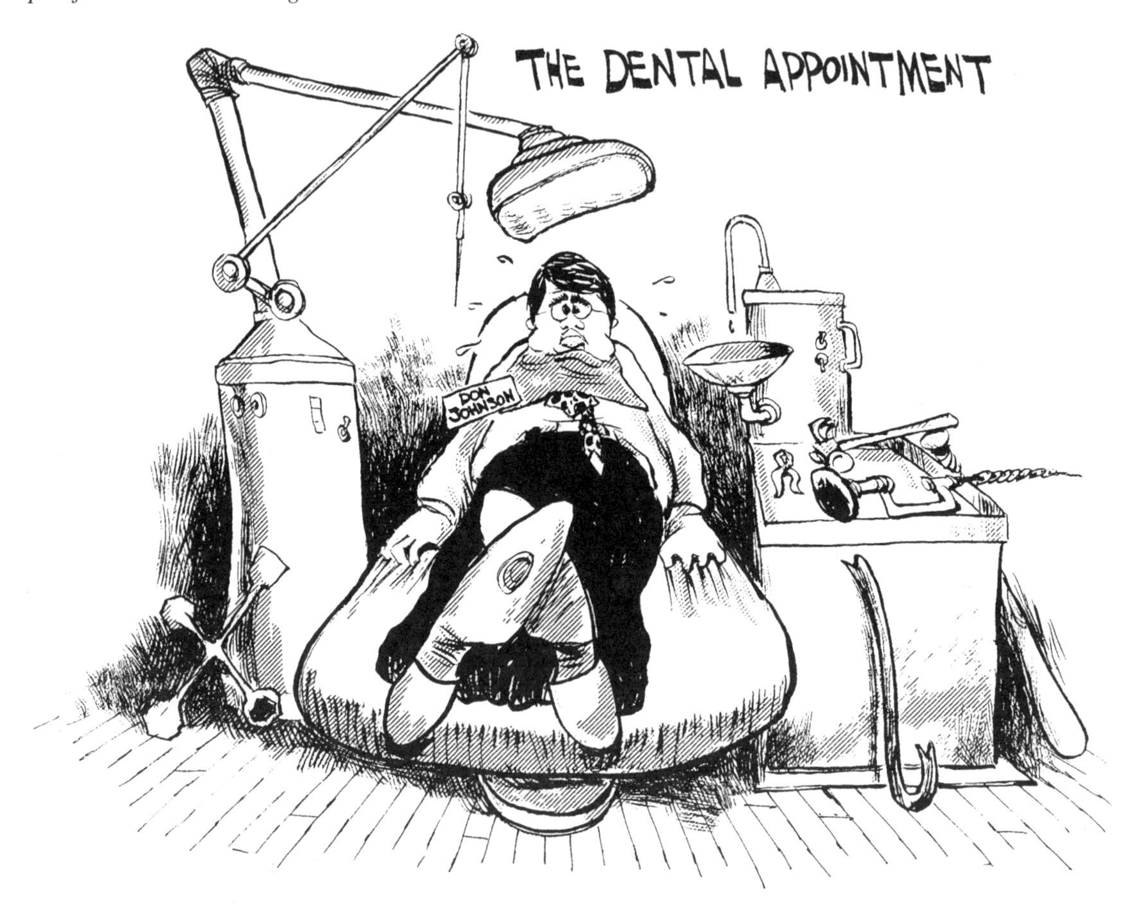

A bellicose and increasingly isolationist North Korea resists the world community's attempts to monitor its stockpile of nuclear weapons.

Polls show the British people are tiring of the antics of their royal family, not to mention their upkeep in terms of tax moneys. U.S. polls show similar feelings toward the ruling Democrats.

Voters give the Republicans control of both houses of Congress for the first time in 40 years.

After months of broken promises, the UN's word doesn't hold water with the Bosnians.

A UN-sanctioned arms embargo serves to restrict arms on only the beleagured Bosnians.

In 1995, the Dayton Accord, refereed by Secretary of State Warren Christopher, was signed by Balkan leaders Izetbegovic and Tudjman. The Bosnian Serbs declared their opposition and Clinton sends 20,000 troops to join a UN contingent in maintaining a shaky peace.

Major League baseball players earn an average of $1.2 million per year. Owners demand a cap on salaries. Impasse! A U.S. delegation led by Jimmy Carter had, at about this time, mediated a somewhat successful solution to an impasse of sorts in Haiti.

The players strike in August, ending the season and for the first time in 84 years, there is no World Series.

The mayor fights another battle against the county: the apportionment of 911 funds.

It comes to light that top officials of University Hospital had used ER treatment and billed it to indigent care (i.e. at taxpayer's expense).

Other expenses of dubious legality surfaced around Christmastime.

A sure sign of serious financial problems, bouncing checks, are denied by the mayor even as they bounce.

As Augusta's population and tax base decline, city leaders refuse to accept their responsibility to either raise taxes or cut spending or both. The alternative is bankruptcy.

To help shoulder the burden, the old standby, water and sewerage rates, are called upon with the major portion carried by the service areas outside the city

All of which is closing the barn door after the horse has galloped away. The gravity of this situation was probably never fully realized by the public. Default by a city of Augusta's size would have been a major story and would have been devastating to the city's prestige and image for years to come. That default was a certainty, a fact denied in later years by some elected city officials, has been verified by those employed by the city to monitor and manage its funds at that time.

After difficulty in meeting the payroll, more than 150 city workers are fired.

More cosmetic than effective, measures such as a crackdown to collect overdue traffic fines are instituted. Among the 'culprits' ferreted out are Augusta Chronicle staffers and Commissioner Lee Neel. It would cost Neel in the next election.

Another stopgap measure is placing city properties on the auction block.

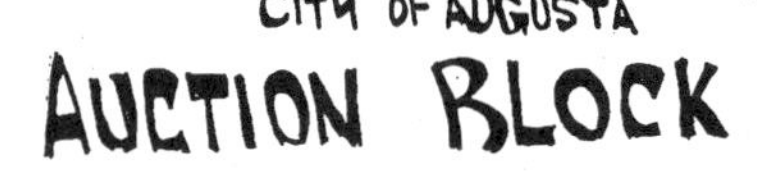

After taking control of both houses of Congress, GOP House Speaker Newt Gingrich takes on the task that Democrats had long neglected — reining in the huge deficits that had reached $250 billion a year.

The new Speaker of the House, conservative Republican Newt Gingrich, draws the attention of the opposition.

The assault on the Christian Coalition from the left goes on. It is one thing to oppose a specific policy or maybe several policies, but to constantly assail an organization as a whole in trying to influence government policies is a little puzzling at times.

A court ruling on re-districting brings histrionics from Cynthia and a contempt of court citation for father Billy.

The Corps of Engineers goes fishing.

COMING UP—
THE FIRST SWINGS OF SPRING TRAINING
OWNERS
PLAYERS

The acrimony of the baseball strike carries over to the 1995 spring training season.

PLAY BALL!

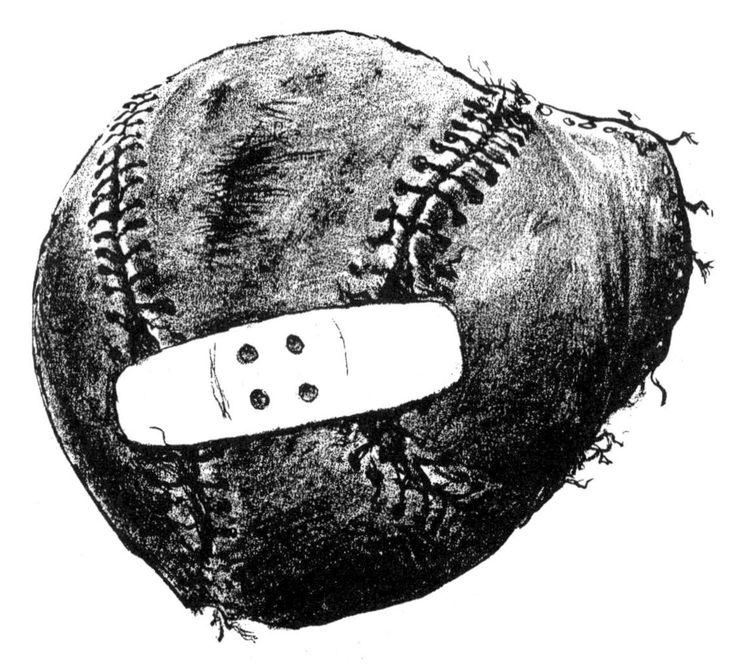

Sensing the disenchantment of fans with their greed and superciliousness, the owners and players come to a shaky agreement and the season begins, a few games late.

Their sense of disenchantment was correct.

Baltimore Oriole Cal Ripken, Jr. surpasses Lou Gehrig's 56-year-old mark by playing in his 2,131st consecutive major league game. Even the fabled Energizer Bunny would have needed a recharge.

Illegal immigration from Mexico escalates as America's booming economy is a magnet to the world.

On April 19, 1995, an explosion ripped apart the Oklahoma City Federal Building. Terrorism had reached America's heartland.

A member of an anti-government splinter group, Timothy McVeigh, is charged as the principle bomber and would be tried and sentenced to die. 169 died in the blast, many of them children, and 500 were injured.

A SPECIAL REMEMBRANCE FOR THE MOTHERS WHO LOST THEIR CHILDREN IN OKLAHOMA CITY.
MOTHERS DAY 1995
WELCH
THE AUGUSTA CHRONICLE

Fashion designer Klein uses younger and younger models in his sexually suggestive commercials and advertisements.

Dan Quayle continues to take shots from the 'Murphy Brown' crowd.

McNamara admits the error of the Vietnam War. Our draft dodging president issues a self-serving statement to the people.

This time, with the support of local black leadership, the Justice Department OKs consolidation – effective date January 1, 1996.

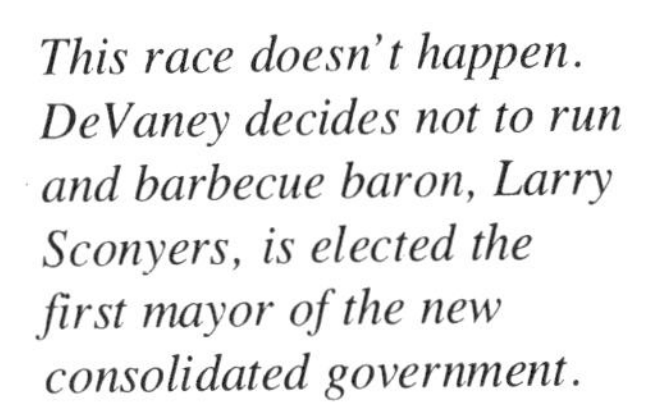
This race doesn't happen. DeVaney decides not to run and barbecue baron, Larry Sconyers, is elected the first mayor of the new consolidated government.

LET THE GAMES BEGIN

CHAIRMAN-MAYOR RACE

CAN ANYONE GIVE AN EXAMPLE OF TODAY'S VOCABULARY WORD?

BUFFOONERY

The Richmond County School Board, evenly divided with five blacks and five whites, has difficulty reaching a consensus on anything. The position of superintendent would remain vacant for over a year before the appointment of Dr. Charles Larke, Richmond County's first black superintendent of schools.

DR. LYNN CADLE CONDUCTS A LESSON ON FREEDOM OF THE PRESS FOR THE SCHOOL CHILDREN OF COLUMBIA COUNTY.
The Augusta Chronicle

Columbia County School Superintendent Dr. Lynn Cadle objects to editorials in the Chronicle and cancels the school system's subscriptions. The subscriptions were renewed a few days later.

For a time, retired general Colin Powell seriously considered a run for the Republican nomination for president. This was of concern in more than one quarter, for he would have been a formidable opponent.

Sam Nunn calls it quits after four outstanding terms — for Georgia and for the country.

Judging from the mail, this cartoon made the two on the left angry.

Celebrations marking the Fiftieth Anniversary of the end of World War II renew hindsight criticism of the dropping of atom bombs on Japan.

Following the Jan Kemp imbroglio, Georgia tilts the playing field by raising academic standards for its athletes above those of most of their opponents. Graduation rates do rise, which is good, but Georgia football suffered, which was not good.

Coach Ray Goff's mediocre career as Georgia football coach would not survive the 1995 season.

Following their termination, Goff and basketball coach Hugh Durham sue the University Athletic Association and receive handsome separation packages.

Shannon Faulkner quits a few days after becoming the first woman to be admitted to The Citadel.

McNeely takes the count a few seconds into the first round.

The O.J. Simpson trial, with TV cameras turning it into a judicial circus, muddles on for nine months.

O.J. and one of his 'dream team' lawyers, Robert Shapiro.

O.J.'s lead attorney, Johnnie Cochran, abetted by LAPD detective Mark Fuhrman, plays the race card, and gets a 'not guilty' verdict despite overwhelming evidence to the contrary.

Following the verdict, many Americans question our system of justice.

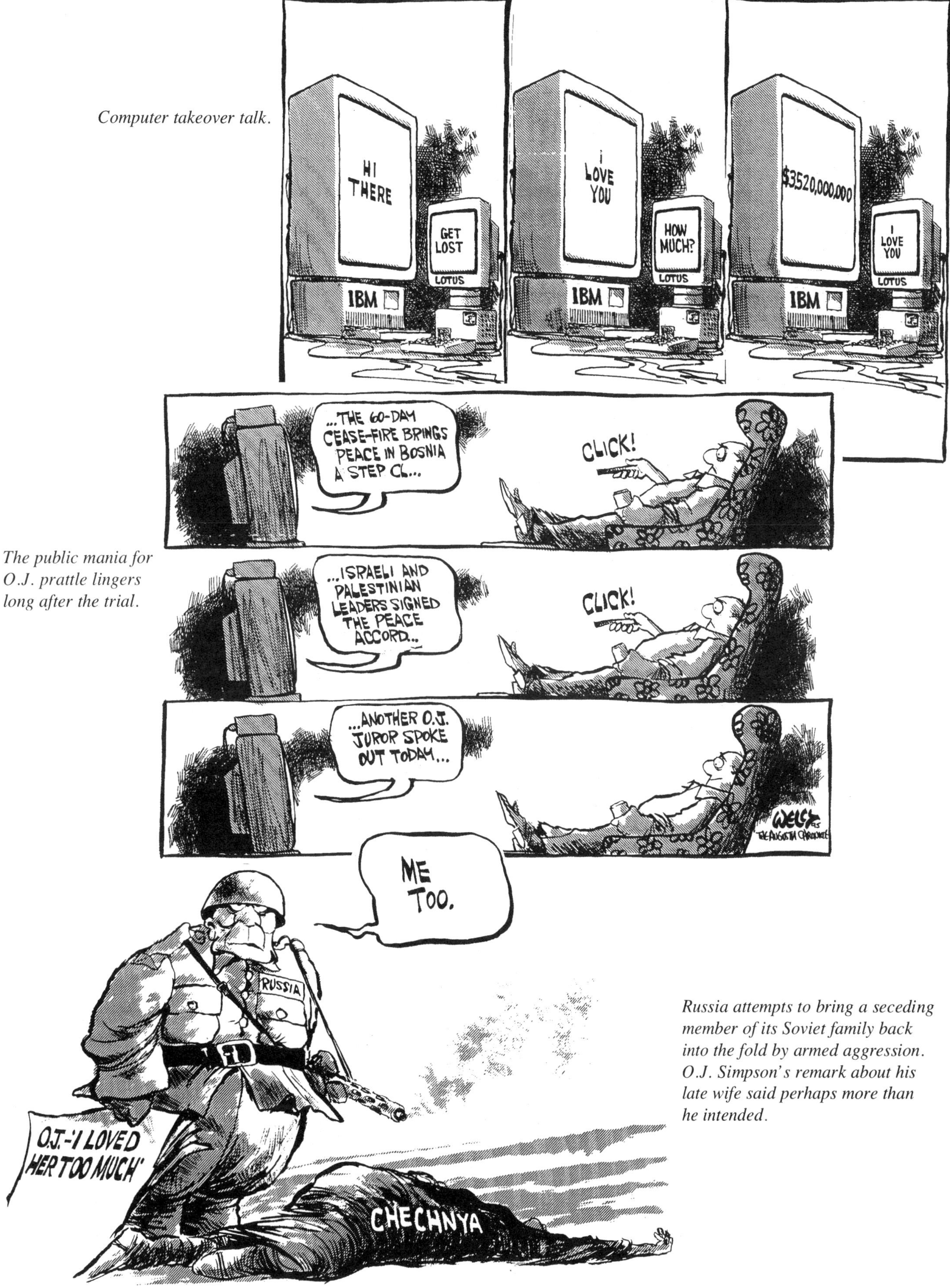

Computer takeover talk.

The public mania for O.J. prattle lingers long after the trial.

Russia attempts to bring a seceding member of its Soviet family back into the fold by armed aggression. O.J. Simpson's remark about his late wife said perhaps more than he intended.

An extended government shutdown over the budget battle leads to the furloughing of non-essential federal workers.

The new government elections produce few new faces.

Bullying and harassment by Coliseum Authority Chairman Ernie Bowman leads to the resignation of manager Wendy Oglesby. The affair would lead to Bowman's ouster and to reforms in the authority's management of the civic center.

Sen. Ernest Hollings, 35 years as Democratic senator from South Carolina, is rewarded for a vote.

Sen. Ernest Hollings

Like his neighboring governor, Zell Miller, South Carolina governor David Beasley decides to change the state of state flag flying. When the dust settled, the Confederate flag was still flying atop the state capitol building.

Alone among the leading countries of the world, France continues the testing of nuclear weapons.

After the GOP gains of 1994, Clinton begins acting more like a Republican than a Democrat.

Rep. Waldholtz's husband and campaign manager effectively ends her congressional career with campaign chicanery and theft. Prince Charles admits to an adulterous affair. Lady Di later admits to the same.

Former Berkeley professor, Ted John Kaczynski, is arrested as the Unabomber. He is charged with making 16 bombs that killed three and injured 23. During this time he issued manifestoes demanding a return to a more primitive standard of living.

Medical research for the cure of AIDS continues to show little promise. One cure for the epidemic has and remains effective.

Perot again wins the nomination of HIS Reform Party and runs for president. He wins 8 percent of the vote, less than half of what he pulled in 1992.

Malfeasance and misfeasance in the Richmond County garage over a period of years — County Administrator Linda Beazley sends former garage director David Rollins to ''investigate'' the sordid mess.

Basic advice from lawyers since the invention of the bar — stall, sit tight and admit nothing.

Lie detectors detect lies but reluctant pursuit by local and state law enforcement officials lead to the conclusion that the foxes had nothing to do with the missing chickens. County taxpayers take a multi-hundred-thousand-dollar hit and life and taxes move on. Meanwhile, Bill and Hillary Rodham see hope in a change of venue.

An area location of golf ball manufacturer Titleist is not helped by freelance industry recruiters.

The biggest sports contract in history brings a pious denial.

Australian Greg Norman charges into Sunday's final Masters round with a 6-shot lead. The ball proved too large and the Great White Shark choked.

England's Nick Faldo is the winner.

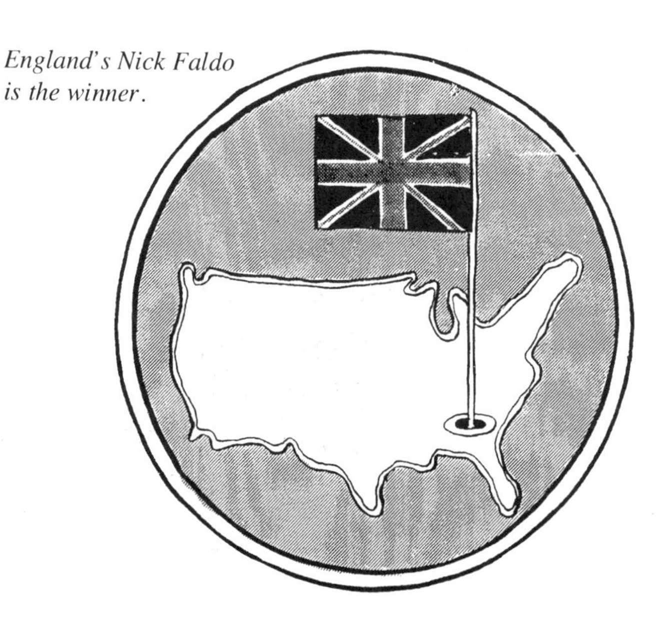

The agony of New Ellenton continues. An assist from the doctor perhaps…

SRS regularly announces layoffs and, on occasion, do indeed lay off a few.

Aiken Police Department is reluctant in releasing public information to the public.

The Olympic flame passes through Augusta on its way to Atlanta.

Mayor Larry's few winks during a commission meeting proves to be a photo-op for a wide awake Chronicle photographer.

An attempt to relocate and upgrade a county department runs into an old roadblock.

Sen. Charles Walker is the new Majority Leader of the Georgia Senate.

Consultant Carstarphen tells elected leaders that if they gave more authority to professional department heads it would produce a more effective and efficient government.

It appears at times that the Whitewater charges, stemming from a failed S&L and real estate dealings in Arkansas by the Clintons, are serious and far-reaching. Several of the principals are jailed in Arkansas.

On May 11, 1996, ValueJet 592 crashed into the Florida Everglades, killing 110 people. The crash was to be blamed on improperly boxed oxygen cannisters but inadequate inspection and maintenance by the super-cheap airline, the FAA and the maintenance operators would be blamed for not overseeing aviation safety.

Pat Buchanan emerges as a strong presidential contender but his far right platform threatens the stability of the Republican challenge.

Sen. Phil Gramm and publisher Steve Forbes drop out after the early primaries show their tax policies have little voter appeal.

AUGUSTA'S OLYMPIC VENUE - TV WATCHING

Despite concerted efforts and strong local connections, Augusta is snubbed by the Olympics.

A bomb explodes in Olympic Park in Atlanta, killing one and injuring several. A security guard, Richard Jewell, comes under FBI suspicion and intense scrutiny by the media.

BEING THE FBI IS NEVER HAVING TO SAY YOU'RE SORRY.

After several months of investigation Jewell is cleared by the FBI. He is successful in reaching financial settlements with two TV networks but no apology is forthcoming from the FBI.

The tarnished image of baseball is further stained when Baltimore 2nd baseman Roberto Alomar spits in the face of an umpire during an argument.

Sweeping welfare reform legislation is passed. Though harshly criticized by many, it promised change in a program that, after 60 years, was not working.

The benefits of the new government are slow in coming…

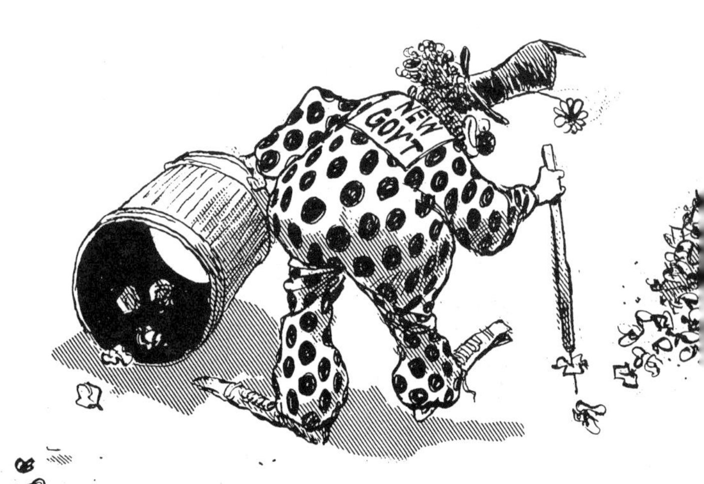

…including the basic service of picking up the trash.

A popular news photo of UGA V attacking an Auburn football player during the overtime win over the Tigers is cast with a different attackee.

Could the flim flams and machinations of the local Irish Traveler community shed some light on the uncollected trash and unkempt cemeteries?

Dole wins the Republican nomination, proposes an across-the-board 15 percent tax cut and selects former football star and congressman Jack Kemp as his running mate.

Sen. Robert Dole

Clinton's campaign rhetoric promises a bridge to the future.

Clinton wins but Dole experiences a professional upgrade from politician to TV pitchman and comedian of sorts.

Mandatory inclusions of presidential character; don't break the law by smoking pot, don't dodge the military draft and don't be a womanizer.

Governor Zell, zigging from his liberal Democratic past, emulates his buddy, the president, by zagging to the right.

China is awarded MFN trade status despite numerous human rights abuses and trade violations.

The Pope announces a visit to atheist and communist Cuba.

Israeli Prime Minister Yitzhak Rabin is assassinated by a militant Israeli in 1995. He had signed the Oslo Accord with Arafat, charting a moderate path toward a Mideast solution between Israel and the Palestinians.

Revelations that foreign money from the Far East, in particular from China to the Democrats, may have influenced U.S. elections.

In the civil trial of O.J. Simpson, he denied ever abusing Nicole despite overwhelming evidence to the contrary. The jury found him responsible for the wrongful deaths of Nicole and her friend, Ronald Goldman.

NEAT CANNON. WHERE'D YOU FIND IT?
THANKS. IT WAS LEFT OVER FROM THE REVOLUTION.
NEWT
HOUSE ETHICS

Speaker Gingrich comes under fire from the House Ethics Committee. He would be fined $300,000 for ethics violations.

Mayor Sconyers wishes an old nemesis, Commissioner Moses Todd, a pleasant journey.

Democrat and wheelchair-bound Secretary of State Max Cleland receives some cheap shots from the Republican side in the 1996 Georgia Senate primary. He would ultimately win the seat vacated by Sam Nunn.

The Easter Seal Center faces eviction to make room for the new Georgia Golf Hall of Fame.

Not too much exaggeration here. Being the only air carrier serving Augusta, Delta has stuck it to Augusta travelers for years.

The annual downtown Longhorn Cattle Drive conflicts with the Super Bowl.

The ball was lost. Titleist decides not to build a plant in the area.

Communication problems have beset local governments for many years.

A sordid affair unfolds at the Medical College of Georgia. Borison and Diamond allegedly pocketed the $10 million and performed sloppy and derelict research on patients for ten years literally under the nose of MCG president Francis Tedesco.

The Clinton White House raised big bucks for the Democratic National Committee by allowing big contributors to spend the night in the Lincoln bedroom at the White House. Gov. Miller spends the night and flies to Augusta with the president, who unveils his national educational initiative at Augusta State University. (The initiative is based on Miller's Hope Scholarship program for Georgia students.)

One of the few times a president has come to Augusta and not played a round of golf.

Welfare reform happens with early positive results. People are going to work for the first time in a long time and feeling better for it.

It's payback time. Zell appointed Tom to the Board of Regents and son, Robert L. Allgood, Superior Court judge.

Congress and the president sign on to a budget that promises a balanced budget with some big 'ifs'. Primarily, the economy must continue booming.

Clinton is sued by Paula Jones, who claims the then Governor Clinton made improper sexual overtures to her in Arkansas. What with Whitewater rippling along, the president's legal bills are mounting. Newt's bill is the $300,000 fine from the House Ethics Committee.

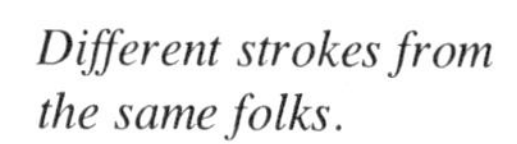
Different strokes from the same folks.

TV 'COMEDY'

I'M ELLEN AND I'M GAY!!

WHEN DO I LAUGH, DAD?

Another sit-com comprising a situation of little comedy.

The theory stems from the fact that a house with a broken window left unrepaired, in time, will further deteriorate, becoming possibly a crack house and a haven for criminal activities. New York City, in particular, has successfully used the theory by arresting miscreants for minor offenses, thus discouraging further, more serious misdeeds. It seems to work as crime has significantly been reduced where it has been implemented.

There is no slumbering for Alan Greenspan, the ever-vigilant chairman of the Federal Reserve Board.

A curious subject, a course in how to take tests, crops up in Georgia's school curriculum.

The racially divided board continues its bickering. Ebonics was a short-lived attempt to adjust educational programs to a black dialect.

Augusta's Charlie Norwood is one of Joe Camel's favorite congressmen.

A part-time sheriff's deputy, fearing an attack from the dog, shoots the pet, Ruben, in its owner's yard. The public is not enchanted with Columbia County Sheriff Clay Whittle's ''shoot first, consider the options later'' policy.

Hometown girl makes good in outer space.

Masters time and badges remain scarce.

Tiger is Eldrick Woods, the Bear is Jack Nicklaus, the Shark Greg Norman, and the Elk is Steve Elkington. The Tiger wins going away, posting a record-shattering score of 270, 18 under par.

Golf legend Ben Hogan is dead.

PHIL NIEKRO WILL BE
INDUCTED INTO THE BASEBALL
HALL OF FAME TODAY.
WITH 318 WINS (268 AS A
BRAVE) THE OLD KNUCKLEBALLER
HAD TO WAIT A RIDICULOUS
FOUR YEARS AFTER BECOMING
ELIGIBLE FOR INDUCTION.
WEEKS

August 3, 1997

SQUEALING LIKE STUCK PIGS

The line-item veto has been a weapon of Georgia's governors in cutting pet projects from bloated budgets…

…and while the president uses the newly-passed law at the federal level for the first time, the cuts are more for show than real.

Georgia's athletic director makes some noise about upgrading the Dawgs weak home schedule, declares defeat and schedules the same old bunch.

Former Georgia Attorney General Mike's admission of an adulterous affair severely weakens his candidacy. Lt. Gov. Pierre drops out leaving former Republican gubernatorial and Senate candidate Guy in the catbird seat.

First man in space and partisan Democratic senator from Ohio, John Glenn teams with Democratic-appointed Attorney General Janet Reno to stall the Senate hearings looking into campaign funding violations. The major violations appear to stem from abuses from within the White House.

Sen. John Glenn

A spate of sexual harassment and misconduct charges in the military lead to resignations and courts-martial.

The gorilla is gone and military base closings could be in Georgia's future.

94 year-old Strom is the Cal Ripken of the Senate…or is Cal the Strom Thurmond of baseball?

STROM THURMOND— AMERICA'S LONGEST-SERVING SENATOR

THE LONE RANGER

The Board of Regents, including good friend Tom Allgood, are not impressed with Dr. Fran's belated efforts to upgrade MCG's research grant oversight program. Anti-depressant medication may possibly be prescribed here. Dr. Borison, call your cellblock.

Healthmaster owner Jeanette Garrison and two underlings receive prison sentences for implementing schemes to defraud Medicare. Much of the money went to Democratic campaign coffers.

Larry's leadership takes the heat.

New county administrator Randy Oliver breathes some fresh air into Richmond County's moribund politics.

Great Britain's Princess Diana is killed in a Paris car crash after attempting to elude an omnipresent band of free-lance photographers known as paparazzi. A few days later Mother Theresa dies following a lifelong crusade aiding the poor of India.

Athens Magazine cover illustration (sans color) depicting Georgia football radio announcer Larry Munson calling the famous Belue-to-Scott TD pass that beat Florida in 1980.

*Sunday comic strip **Go Figure** (sans color)*

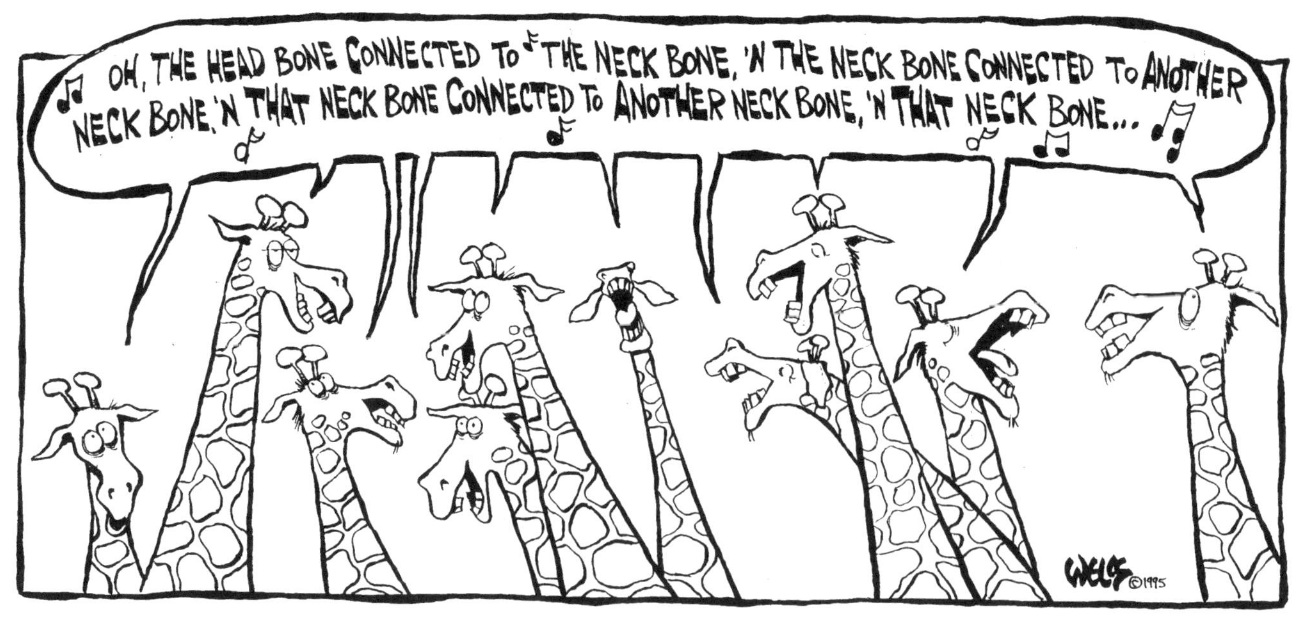

9-17
AND THEN THERE WAS HERMAN, WHO REALLY DIDN'T GIVE A RIP THAT THE GRASS WAS GREENER ON THE OTHER SIDE.
WEISS ©1995
MUNCH MUNCH
BURP

HERMAN CONTINUED TO BE AMUSED BY THE PHILOSOPHICAL MUSINGS OF OTHERS, NOT TO MENTION THE DIETARY ADVANTAGES, OF IGNORING THE GREENER GRASS ON THE OTHER SIDE... UNTIL THAT FATEFUL, SUMMER MORNING...
BEEF INC. Meat Packers
9-24
MUNCH MUNCH
BURP
WEISS ©1995
TO BE CONT'D.

THE SAGA OF HERMAN-THE CONCLUSION
BEEF INC.
10-1
IT WAS LATER LEARNED DURING HERMAN'S PRE-BUTCHERY CHECKUP THAT HE WAS NEITHER A GLUTTONOUS DEVIATE, NOR WAS HE DEVOID OF AN INNATE YEARNING FOR THE GREENER GRASS ON THE OTHER SIDE. TRAGICALLY, HE WAS COLOR-BLIND!
WEISS ©1995

MONTHS AT SEA AND ALL THE FRESH VEGETABLES AND FRUIT ARE GONE...
WELLS ©1995
...BUT WILL MY LADS FALL PREY TO OL' DEMON SCURVY?... FILLIN' SICK BAY WITH TEETH AFALLIN' OUT...
7-30
NO!! STOREKEEP, BREAK OUT THE VITAMIN C I ORDERED ABOARD AFORE WE SAILED!
VITAMIN B

TOADYING UP TO LOUIS XIV—THE SUN KING!
11-5
WELLS ©1995

GAUL 51 B.C. JULIUS CAESAR INTRODUCES THE SIX-SECOND SOUND BITE.
10-22
VENI! VIDI! VICI!
WELLS ©1995

NEW YORK CITY, 1868. YOUNG WILLIAM F. CODY CALLS ON A MADISON AVENUE IMAGE CONSULTANT FIRM.
WARTHOG BILL!! WARTHOG BILL!! JUST BECAUSE I SHOOT AN OCCASIONAL WARTHOG, THEY CALL ME WARTHOG BILL!.. WHY, IT'S DOWNRIGHT EMBARRASSING!!
HAVE YOU CONSIDERED SHOOTING BUFFALOS?
WEISS ©1995

LADY GODIVA MEETS THE EMPEROR WITH NO CLOTHES.
TSK, TSK.!..
My, My.!..
WEISS ©1995 9-3

TEARING HIS MASK DURING THEIR LATEST ADVENTURE, THE LONE RANGER SENDS IT BY TONTO INTO TOWN TO BE MENDED. RARELY SEEN, TONTO'S LATENT SENSE OF HUMOR SURFACES. NEITHER THE RANGER NOR SILVER ARE AMUSED WITH THE TEMPORARY REPLACEMENT DISGUISE!
WEISS ©1995

Last cartoon